This I Call to Mind

Dear Roy

~ Many great memories!

~ Thanks for everything

& very Best wishes

Anthony

Oct. 2018

Dedication

*With thanks as ever to Philip Ralli,
the publisher, to family, friends,
students, colleagues, and listeners
in many contexts, who patiently
put up with these selections being
considered as they all-too-slowly
took shape.*

*Your forbearance and
kindness are inspirational.*

This I Call
to Mind

Anthony Buckley

First published in 2017 by Highland Books, 2 High Pines, Knoll Road, Godalming, GU7 2EP, England

ISBN-13: 978-1-897913-95-6

ISBN-10: 1-897913-95-8

Ebook ISBN: 978-1-909690-95-0

Printed in the UK by CPI Books

Contents

Yet this I call to mind
... And therefore
I have hope

It was a difficult time.

The context was this: In the 6th century BC it seemed as if everything was falling apart for the people of Israel. Expectations were dashed, the enemies had arrived and conquered, first the Northern Kingdom and then the Southern – the defeat of the Israelites was total. The future looked uncertain and full of loss.

This sentence *"Yet this I call to mind and therefore I have hope"* is taken from Lamentations, a short book found in ancient Jewish scriptures and later included in what Christians call the Old Testament. It was time to lament and the writer has one weapon left – he (it probably was a 'he', and might well have been the great prophet Jeremiah) still has his *mind*. His heart may be broken but his mind is only bruised. And so he 'calls to mind', calls *into* his mind, something that will help.

It takes effort to 'call to mind', especially when the lamenting is loud. The implication is that there is truth outside the current noise that needs to be called in, that may not be there automatically, that needs to be intentionally invited in to join the discussion round the table. Our minds can sometimes become full of storms and confusion, uncertainties and despair, and there may seem little room for anything else. Jeremiah makes the effort, he calls into mind truths that change how he feels about the situation, that will quieten the other voices.

"Yet this I call to mind" he continues *"And therefore* I have hope" The need to have hope runs very deep in human nature. If we can be sure that there is light at the end of the road then it is much easier to keep travelling. But the hope must be grounded and the writer gives specific reasons why it is justified. "Because of the Lord's great love we are not consumed, for his compassions never fail. They are new every morning" and then turns his reflection to praise: "Great is your faithfulness" What does he call to mind? That the love of God will see him safely through, that the mercy of God never fails and is offered fresh, revitalising, every morning. There is sure ground for hope, the faithfulness of God is completely reliable. Therefore he has hope, even though everything seems to be falling apart.

The verse, Lamentations 3:21, has been quoted, memorised and pondered through the centuries. It is a reminder that the Bible is full of phrases or sentences which can reach deep inside us, can stop us in our tracks. Here are words which can change our feelings or behaviours, whatever our journey. The tracks we follow run through a varied and sometimes uncharted landscape, and we respond as we are. The sunset that causes one traveller to stop and smile may leave another untouched. The glimpse of a rainbow that causes an intake of breath today may not do the same tomorrow. Our poignant sigh at a sudden view of an island meets no response in our companion; their attention may be on another vista, bringing a different echo, more personal to them. Their journey is not the same as ours.

Here is a selection of phrases, from the library of books that we now call the Bible, that have often caused me to pause. Anyone familiar with the Bible will note different phrases that carry significance; for those new to the Bible and who want to know more about it, perhaps the background of some of these phrases will be of interest. We are stopped in our tracks so that the journey will continue in a slightly different way, we travel onwards as changed people.

To keep the length manageable, I have chosen to draw mostly from the narratives in the Bible, whether story or history. There is thus little reference to the Old Testament Law, Wisdom and Prophetic books, or to the New Testament letters.

Some of the phrases have literary power in themselves. (The documents that were collected together to form the Bible are very old; the original skill that ensures the words still speak today after more than two millennia is in itself worth considering.) Some of the phrases seem ordinary but the context brings drama to the words. Some may stop us in our tracks because they raise a smile, others because they inspire. Some through their poignancy, others through their challenge.

These are brief reflections, nothing more. They are not designed to provoke or convert, simply to encourage further thoughts in any who may read them. And especially, following Jeremiah's example, to encourage hope. They are not uniformly cheerful; true hope is not found in a relentlessly upbeat patter, but rather in a deepening understanding that there is a higher reality, a richer story, than the purely physical and the self-interested. I would recommend spacing out the reading of the following reflections, to allow time to question what the phrase signifies for you, and to allow the noise of the author's clumsy comments to fade so that your own thoughts are the ones that stick.

Six centuries after Jeremiah, in a personal ending to his letter of encouragement for Timothy, a leader in the early church, Paul, asked for "my scrolls, especially the parchments". He knows that he is under a death sentence, that the finishing line is drawing near, but he is determined to press on in thinking, to keep on reading, so he really needs his scrolls. (He also wants his cloak, it must have been cold in prison.)

It is good to build our personal library of wisdom that can be visited, recalled, browsed in, whatever the weather. Jeremiah knows what is truly worth calling to mind; Paul wants his parchments with him. We no longer use scrolls; we have books and electronic devices. May our desire to learn wisdom be equal to theirs.

Anthony Buckley, Summer 2017

—1—

Genesis 3:9
(Genesis 3:1-10 for the context)

"Where are you?"

This is the first question that God asks in the Bible. He asks it to Adam and Eve, to man and woman, to humanity. He is asking it while "walking in the garden in the cool of the day."

The setting is one of beauty; it speaks of rest, peace and relationship. Who would not wish to be part of this strolling through Eden as the sun slowly sets?

Adam and Eve do not wish to be part of it. Humanity is hiding.

Where are you?

This question sums up all that the sixty-six books of the Bible want to say about God and humanity. The narrator is saying that God wants to be with us, he wants us to be with him. As simple as that.

Where are you?

Later writers will talk about Jesus coming "to *seek* and save what was lost." Jesus will tell stories about the shepherd who had lost the sheep, the woman who had lost the coin, the father who had lost the son, and how they walked, searched, found, watched, ran and embraced. And then rejoiced at the reconciliation.

Adam and Eve know they have chosen to hide, to reposition themselves outside the beauty and the peace. They have decided to hear the tempter's voice asking "Did God really say?" instead of the primary, creative, sustaining voice they had originally heard, the voice full of unfathomable wisdom and relentless love. They know what God has said, they have chosen to ignore it.

("Did God really say?" is the first question of all in the Bible, and that placing by the narrator has its own significance.)

What causes us to want to hide? Perhaps we are frightened to be seen as we are and have worked hard to stitch together many figurative fig leaves to cover our vulnerabilities. It may be the fear of letting go of imagined independence and control, it may be the fear of being challenged about some of our attitudes and behaviour. The emotional and searching intimacy of love may be too much of a challenge.

Where are you?

Many, many, years later a thief is being crucified outside the walls of Jerusalem. One of countless people, some innocent and some guilty, who died in this way. He turns to the man being crucified next to him and pleads "Jesus, remember me." Jesus replies: "Today you will be with me in paradise." The Greek word translated as paradise is "garden". All that Eden represents is being restored.

But humanity's tendency to hide, from God and from one another, has not yet gone away.

But God still comes looking.

Chapter —1

—2—

Genesis 4:9
(Genesis 4:1-10 for the context)

"Am I my brother's keeper?"

Another question... and the different ways that this question has been answered is the history of humanity. The answering of this question is the story of every relationship, of every family and of every community.

Cain has killed his brother. Abel's sacrifice to God had been accepted, Cain's had not. We are not told why, as if the storyteller is reminding us that this is none of our business, best rather that we focus on checking the integrity of our own attitudes. Instead of searching his own soul to work through the problem, Cain's jealousy takes over and he murders his brother. He then tries to deflect the question "Where is your brother?" with the careless "Am I my brother's keeper?"

But perhaps it is not careless. Perhaps it is a genuine attempt to draw limits to his responsibility for others.

The answer is so obvious that the storyteller does not supply it. With dramatic effect the question is left hanging so that the hearers feel they must commit to providing the answer themselves.

Am I my brother's and sister's keeper? Yes.

Am I my brother's and sister's keeper? Yes, we are born into community, with the responsibilities of relationships. We are entwined and interlinked.

Cain has broken the link. Jealousy turning to murder is an understandable but terrible progression: If we are jealous of someone, we wish that the part that we envy in them is wiped away, we wish it dead. The more the jealousy grows, the larger the desire to wipe away grows. Cain no longer sees Abel as a brother, he now sees him as a rival.

Cain knows he has done wrong, otherwise he would not have troubled to bury the body.

It is God who challenges Cain about the care of his brother. It is God whose gaze Cain tries to avoid by asking a different question in return. And it is God who knows what Cain is hiding.

It is foolish of Cain to think that God does not know: honesty and repentance are always preferable to denial and, in the long term, much less costly. But in the moment of guilt and fear this is easy to forget.

It feels much easier to isolate oneself from

any sense of responsibility for others and for the effects of our actions.

Am I my brother's keeper?

The fact that Cain thought it appropriate to ask the question is worrying. And continues to be so.

—3—

"He brought out
bread and wine"

The phrase is ordinary enough, but the context is full of mystery and the echoes run through the millennia, in fact are heard several times each day, somewhere in the world.

A person called Melchizedek appears from Salem, the old name for Jerusalem. He is a priest and a king and brings bread and wine. He is meeting Abraham (at that point called Abram), revered to this day by Jews, Muslims and Christians as a person of great faith and vision who left his homeland of Ur to seek new beginnings and to found a new nation. Abraham, father of the faithful, acknowledges spiritual authority in Melchizedek, and gives him a tenth of all he has. Melchizedek accepts this homage and blesses Abraham.

Abraham is fully aware that he has a significant and historic role but he does not try and grasp precedence. He acknowledges that he is in the presence of someone greater than him. He is humble, gracious and generous.

No more is said. This incident is recorded in the Genesis story with no explanation or interpretation. And then about two thousand years later there is a carpenter's son in Jerusalem, whom people are acclaiming as priest and king. And he is offering bread and wine. And he is blessing people.

The mystery of Melchizedek must have been much discussed and pondered by the Jewish people. Who was he? Why was he included in the narrative? Why no explanation? The writer of the letter to the Hebrews in the New Testament assumes that his readers know about him and then unhesitatingly affirms that in some way Melchizedek foreshadowed Jesus.

He brought out bread and wine

Bread and wine speak of nourishment and refreshment, of giving and receiving. Together. They speak of hospitality and generosity. Here is a Priest King who wishes to welcome us, to feast us, to renew us. Holy Communion, The Mass, The Eucharist, The Lord's Supper – whatever titles are given to this Christian ceremony which has been celebrated daily for nearly two thousand years, it is helpful to remember the central simplicity and richness of bread and wine, and who is offering it.

Sometimes things may happen which appear to make no sense and which are not explained. The Melchizedek story is shrouded in mystery but is a reminder that there will come a day when the bigger picture will give meaning to the unexpected shape and colouring of the piece of the jigsaw that currently appears so inexplicable.

And if there is an experience that seems to speak of an existence bigger than the purely material, an encounter which suddenly feels richer than words can express, a meal which seems surprisingly significant, an unexpected desire to respond with generosity, then perhaps this is a Melchizedek moment, that there is something in this ordinary moment that is pointing towards something larger and deeper.

He brought out bread and wine
And we are still talking about it.

—4—

"I will not let you go unless you bless me"

The reckoning was coming. Jacob, who had manipulated and cheated his brother Esau all those years ago, was now having to meet him the next day. This was when it all might come to an end. He prays desperately and sends his family and flocks ahead of him over the river, hoping to soften the expected vengeance of his older brother with gifts and the smiles of others. He does not risk going first; he wants to see how Esau will react. He waits on his own through the long night, with his own thoughts, his own regrets, his own fears.

And there Jacob is wrestled. If you are being wrestled you are held too close to run away. You can choose between collapsing and wrestling, but you cannot escape to prepare, plot and conspire one more time. And you cannot think about a great deal else, either. At some point during this long night he senses that this wrestling is a struggle that matters, that something profound is going on, that this is no ordinary conflict. And then he senses that unbelievably this wrestler is in some way an expression of God himself. He faces the growing realisation that the most important thing seems to be that the mysterious wrestler blesses him. After that, he can go back to his planning and reflecting. After that he can go and see his family are safe. After that, he can go and face Esau. But before he crosses the river, he needs to know that God blesses him, that Jacob, who has got so much wrong, is still part of the divine plan, still part of the family, son of Isaac, grandson of Abraham. He holds on to the wrestler, he does not collapse.

I will not let you go unless you bless me

A wound comes with the wrestling. Jacob's vulnerability and weakness will be evident to all from this night onwards. There will be no more hiding that this is a less than perfect person. There will be no more thinking that through his manipulation and cunning, Jacob can out-God God, shaping his own destiny in his own way. Jacob knows he has been wounded but this is less important than receiving the blessing. That has become the thing that matters.

Jacob has held on while being held. He has not given up and slumped helplessly. And so he is told "(You) have overcome."

We seek approval and affirmation from many different voices. Perhaps before the long night began Jacob was so preoccupied that the only comforting words he thought he needed to hear would be those from his wronged-brother Esau. As morning breaks he knows that they are still important, he still has to go across the river and face his past. But he now knows, and has proved to himself that he knows, that the voice of God, the blessing of God, is the voice that truly matters. He wants to know he is on the right journey. Without that, the other voices, even Esau's, do not reach his deepest needs.

This new ordering of priorities is so significant that it is almost like a new birth, so he is given a new name, Israel.

It is a new beginning. He crosses the river.

And the meeting with Esau goes rather well.

—5—

"Let my people go"

It has become the cry of freedom though the ages and was first heard by a shepherd in a desert as a command he had to pass on to someone else. The someone else, the Pharaoh himself of Egypt, was the most powerful person in that part of the world. The shepherd, Moses, could only look back on what was increasingly appearing to be a life of missed opportunity caused by his own mistakes. He had not always been a shepherd but as a young man a dramatic career change had been needed and life as a prince in an Egyptian palace had been replaced by watching over sheep. It had all begun with a wonderful sign that God was watching over him, when as a vulnerable Israelite baby he had been adopted into the Egyptian royal family. All that had been thrown away. He had thrown it away.

And now life has passed him by and he is getting old. But then he hears a voice calling his name and he is told to take off his shoes because he is on holy ground. The voice identifies itself as belonging to the God of his forefathers: Abraham, Isaac and Jacob. Moses is being reminded that he is part of a much bigger story, and he is told that now is the time to act. And this is not a small, tribal, deity who speaks, this is the God who is ultimate and complete existence. This is 'I am who I am'.

Let my people go

The Israelites were enslaved in Egypt. Initially they had been treated well but new pharaohs had come and gone who "did not know about Joseph", the son of Jacob and the great and respected ancestor of the present generation. The past was the past, attitudes changed and the regime had grown mistrustful and fearful and – it often follows from fear – increasingly spiteful.

Moses had heard the voice of God saying that all that is done is noticed, and this is a God who is on the side of the poor and oppressed and will act: "I have seen, I have heard. I will come down."

Let my people go

Moses does not want to do this. But the calling is there and will not be ignored.

Many years before Moses had reacted impulsively to the ill-treatment of an Israelite slave in Egypt. He had killed the Egyptian and as a result had to flee into the wilderness. Those earlier efforts to 'let my people go' had ended up in shame, dishonour, murder and exile. Going back would be to risk his life and return to a scene of failure. Perhaps he does not want to revisit the place where these old emotional wounds were born. He provides a series of excuses – I stammer a lot, they won't listen to me, isn't there someone else?

God does not relent. This is the calling that Moses must now undertake. He provides what is needed, including the company of Aaron, Moses' brother. He makes no promises to sort our Moses' afflictions, he does not wait for people to be 'perfect' before he uses them. Because there are people in need. This is about a task that must be done and be done quickly. Slavery in its worst and most obvious sense was and is an endemic problem. But there are also unspoken slaveries, people oppressed and trapped by controlling bullies in work or at home.

Whatever the story of our life, whatever the successes, mistakes and missed opportunities, it is good to be alert to the voice of God saying "Go and tell x, let my people go." Moses heard, and after some discussion, obeyed. History was changed.

—6—

"Be strong and courageous"

Moses was an extraordinary person. He faced down Pharaoh. He succeeded in leading his people from slavery in Egypt, in leading through long years of travelling and learning together and to the edge of the promised land itself. He got as far as Mount Nebo and looked over to the new territory, wondering how the next chapter for the people of Israel would read, and then died.

Joshua was chosen to take over. He was a young man following in the footsteps of one of the most inspirational leaders in history. There was no time to consolidate and settle; the invasion of the promised land was impending and this was the time to move forward. He is painfully, bluntly, reminded that "Moses my servant is dead." He needs to begin to accept the reality of grief and to move his people forward, there is a new page to be written and it needs to be written quickly.

Joshua feels, rather understandably, bereft, nervous and inadequate.

He hears God saying *Be strong and courageous.*

And then the same phrase again a few sentences later.

Be strong and courageous

In case the message is not clear, it is then turned around.

Do not be terrified, do not be discouraged.

The implication of this repetition is that Joshua is deeply in need of encouragement, that he is terrified and that he wants to give up. But he is the leader, however scared he feels. This is the calling, however fearful the future may seem. He has to hold on to hope and keep moving.

The three-times encouragement is intermingled with specific wisdom. There is the reminder to take seriously the teachings that have been received in the long journey through the wilderness. The promise that God would bless the move forward: "I will give you every place where you set your foot," with the implication that staying still is not to be considered. The assurance that God will not leave him forsaken, Joshua will not travel alone.

Joshua sets out to lead his people into the Promised Land, mindful of the need to keep the commandments, to keep moving and that God goes with him. Morality, vision and faith are powerful weapons to carry as a person begins a new stage of their journey. The original hearers of this narrative would have marked the importance of hearing and receiving good encouragement, thrice-given, and the need to be good encouragers to others.

Be strong and courageous

Do we say it often enough, and do we hear it when it is said to us?

—7—

Judges 1:15
(Judges 1:11-15 for the context)

"Give me also
springs of water"

The story goes on. The Israelites were settling the land. Caleb, the veteran warrior and friend of Joshua, had given his daughter Acsah in marriage to his nephew Othniel because Othniel had captured an area called Debir.

Acsah was a woman who knew her own mind, knew what was needed and knew her father. The narrator, with an eye for details that help to paint a picture, tells us that "she got off her donkey" and with respect and affection she waits.

"What can I do for you?" her old father asks. He had been one of the first to enter this land many years before, trusted friend of Joshua himself, and has an unrivalled reputation for courage and loyalty.

She answers "Do me a special favour. Since you have given me land in the Negev, give me also springs of water."

31   Chapter —7—

Give me also springs of water

Land itself is not enough. A large area may look impressive, but it will be of little value without life-giving water. Caleb responds by giving her the upper and lower springs.

It must have been a poignant moment for him. His daughter is showing the wisdom and poise that would be needed as the next chapter unfolds. From generation to generation, this is a family who can think clearly.

It is easy to fill lives with the equivalent of land – possessions, accolades, money, achievements – but without spiritual vitality running through them, they will not bear fruit. There is a difference between worldly cleverness in accumulating 'things' and wisdom in knowing that renewed spiritual and emotional refreshing waters are needed. Springs sometimes run below the land as well as above it. However barren the land may look from the surface, if the springs are there then fruit will come.

Water is one of the most important symbols in the Bible. It speaks of life, of baptism, of new beginnings and cleansing. Jesus speaks of himself as the living water, who can satisfy all our thirsts.

Acsah is wise enough to know what is needed and to know the limits of what she can do in her own strength. She knows she cannot create the water herself, nor that it would be sensible to try and struggle on without it, pretending all is well.

She asks for the water, and it is given.

She gets down from her donkey and humbly stands before her father and asks for water. Perhaps for some this can be a helpful picture of prayer.

Give me also springs of water

Springs, not ponds. Acsah wants water that is on the move, always new and always flowing.

Bringing life.

–8–

"There are still too
many men"

Numbers are not everything. The land continued to be settled but control swayed between the Israelites and other tribes. In the time of Gideon, the Midianites held power. Gideon believed he might be called to lead a rebellion, but like Moses before him was unsure that he was the right person and put out a fleece or two to test this. He needs considerable reassurance but finally accepts the calling and begins to gather some forces.

It is a popular cause and many flocked to join Gideon, as the preparations get underway he hears God's voice:

There are still too many men

Gideon reduces the size of his army but is told that there are still too many. Gideon reduces it further. The original army of about thirty-two thousand comes down to about three hundred.

The criteria for the reduction are these: those who are trembling with fear can go home and then those who kneel to drink from the river rather than those who stay standing and scooping up the water with their hands should likewise go. The first reason is clearer than the second, but perhaps there is something in the scooping rather than the kneeling which means that these fighters are still alert, still watchful and ready to move.

Gideon leads his small army carefully and skilfully and the Midianites are defeated. A lesson is learnt about focused commitment, about quality not quantity, about courage and alertness. And there are echoes of another theme that frequently recurs in these narratives: avoid the temptation to be like other nations. Do not rely on what they rely on, whether it is large numbers or tribal gods. The Israelites' strength is to be in their God, not worldly power. At this time of the rule by 'the judges' (including such varied characters as Gideon, Deborah and Samson) the cry to be like others will end up being focused on imitating other nations by asking for a king.

Historically there is military wisdom in preparing a committed few rather than massing large crowds. There is emotional skill in avoiding the temptation to be like others and tactical skill in not expecting simple volume to achieve victory. There may be something to ponder about personal lives and organisations having the confidence not to be over-cluttered with unnecessary activities.

There are still too many men

There is courage and cost in this focusing; the stripping back can be painful and unsettling. What needs to be stored in the background or left behind altogether? What do we truly need for the tasks that face us now, not those that faced us ten years ago? For Gideon, the heart of the issue was whether he and his people could trust God for the future, whether this was where his hope could safely lie.

—9—

Jonah 2:1
(Jonah 1-4 for the context)

"From inside the fish"

It had all gone very wrong. Jonah had refused to go and preach to Nineveh. He had, literally, run from his calling, clambered on a boat, sailed away, hit a storm, admitted to the sailors that he was fleeing from God and was probably more trouble than he was worth, was thrown off the boat and swallowed by a big fish.

We note in passing Jonah's honesty with the sailors. He has the courage and integrity to own up that he is at fault.

From inside the fish, he prays. Not a lot else to do, it could be argued, and often it is difficult times that can lead to the most heartfelt prayers. There are times when we feel swallowed up by a situation and it feels very likely that we will be consumed. As he admits "When my life was ebbing away, I remembered you, Lord."

From inside the fish Jonah prayed to the Lord his God

It is the first time in the story that Jonah talks

to God. God has talked to him but we are only told that Jonah ran away from that voice. It is now, in the midst of disaster, that Jonah talks to God.

In his prayer he is honest about the situation: "seaweed was wrapped around my head" (we can happily picture the storyteller giving this phrase suitable drama, no doubt much to the delight of his younger listeners). But he has hope: "Yet I will look again at your holy temple." The 'again' reminds him of former good times, whilst looking forward to restoration.

In the whale Jonah does not lapse into self-pity or despair, he prays.

He is then released from the whale and the task is renewed. He obediently goes to Nineveh. His ministry there is so effective that even the king repents. People are sometimes unexpectedly struck powerfully when truth is spoken plainly to them, and this is one of the key lessons of this story. The storyteller is a master of his craft and does not stop at this moment of triumph. He goes on to portray Jonah struggling emotionally with this evidence of the love and mercy of God to others, even though he had received so much mercy himself. He is reminded that he is not in charge and rather too easily makes a fuss, after all, he is not in control even of the amount of shade he receives. Sometimes lessons about humility and mercy have to be learned and deepened again and again. If it is right for him to cry from the depths of the whale then it is right for others, including those outside his own cultural community like the king of Nineveh.

Jonah is a grumpy, effective and needy person. An unlikely hero, but at the heart of the story is someone who was prepared to pray in the middle of feeling completely overwhelmed.

From inside the fish Jonah prayed to the Lord his God

When we are using our heart it does not matter where we are praying. The inside of a fish will do as well as a cathedral. And who knows what the results may be.

Ruth 1:16
(Ruth 1-4 for the context)

"Where you go, I will go"

The words of a character strong enough to get into the history books. We do not know if the Jonah expedition, referenced in the last chapter, is historical; it may be, people have survived being swallowed by whales, but it lacks the usual literary marks of being placed in an historical context. The story of Ruth is more clearly written as historical narrative.

Where you go, I will go

It is an unexpected and unnecessary promise and it is one that becomes enormously significant.

Widowed mother-in-law Naomi, in bitter grief, is going back home to Bethlehem. Her husband and her sons had died in Moab, where the family had travelled when harvests failed at home. The famine in Bethlehem was over and Naomi might as well go back. It makes sense for her to go alone, her Moabite daughters-in-law should stay in their homeland and begin again. Orpah, courteous and full of common sense, agrees. Ruth does not. I'm going to Bethlehem with you.

Where you go, I will go

The very brief 'book' now known as Ruth is a narrative with strong characters and much sadness, filled with grief and generosity, humour and hope. The last word in the story would have been the punchline for those early listeners, so important that it has been flagged up a few sentences before.

This last word is 'David'. Sharp intake of breath, or perhaps gentle smiles of satisfaction, from those gathered round the campfire listening to this tale.

Because of Ruth, Boaz has a son, Obed, and two generations later we get to David. The great shepherd king David. Without Ruth, would Israel have had David? Without her promise and her faithfulness, would history have been very different?

It is Ruth's loyalty that is at the heart of the story. She is committed to Naomi and will not pull away from that commitment. After the death of her husband and sons Naomi goes back to Bethlehem understandably heart-broken; Ruth's presence gives company and, in time, comfort and hope. Naomi begins to look to the future and the needs of others as well as herself. She focuses on winning (some would say happily and indulgently match-making) her kinsman Boaz as a husband for Ruth. Boaz is attracted to Ruth but insists on acting honourably, he is the other hero in the story. If he is to marry Ruth then he wants all the formalities and legalities observed, including ensuring that a closer kinsman has the opportunity properly to renounce his claim to her.

Where you go, I will go

Keeping promises of love and commitment is always costly because some other freedom of action will be given up for the promise to be fulfilled. Other desires will need to be put to one side and other opportunities will need to be declined. Naomi was not always (for very understandable reasons) the easiest person to be with, but Ruth sticks with her.

Ruth's sacrificial loyalty is honoured by God and this small family changes history. Did Mary, mother of Jesus, have Ruth's story on her mind as she travelled to Bethlehem, David's town, hundreds of years later, obedient, committed and not quite sure what the future held? Joseph her betrothed was of David's and thus of Ruth's line. Without Ruth, they would not have been going to Bethlehem at all.

—11—

1 Samuel 3:10
(1 Samuel 3:1-21 for the context)

"Speak, for your servant is listening"

Samuel had twice missed the voice of God in the night, mistaking it for the voice of his elderly mentor Eli. But Eli knew better and told the child to stay alert and stay listening. Samuel does, and next time he hears the voice he responds with these words.

Speak, for your servant is listening

These are brave words to say (and the message that Samuel was then given to pass on to Eli was indeed a difficult one to have to say, calamity was to come on the old man's family). But Samuel, guided by Eli, knew that there was no point in asking God to speak if he was not prepared to listen.

Perhaps after the first two times Eli had not been able to get back to sleep either. Young Samuel was certainly hearing something, unless he was dreaming. Perhaps the time had come

43

when God would be doing great things in the next generation and Eli's role would turn from mentor to supporter. Perhaps Eli is not too surprised when Samuel came rushing in the third time. Now is the time to encourage his protégé to take a step; he tells Samuel what to say and to listen for the voice of God. Eli is not going to get in the way, he is not precious about his own standing or status. If God has plans for this young boy then Eli will encourage, not deflect.

Samuel, who listens to Eli and is willing to be obedient to God, will grow up to be the key spiritual figure in Israel of his time. He will be the one who anoints Saul, the first king. He will be the one who anoints David, the second and the greatest king, and in that anointing he again is alert to God's voice unexpectedly choosing the young shepherd boy rather than his more majestic older brothers.

Many years earlier, Samuel's mother Hannah had been faithful, thankful and honourable in her prayers and in her promises; she had not been possessive over her longed-for son and had committed him to God's service. Before Samuel was born she had experienced teasing from her husband's other wife, adding to the profound sorrow of her childlessness. But she had stayed faithful in her praying and in her tears. Eli had misunderstood her distress and assumed she was drunk, but quickly became sympathetic when he heard what was on her heart.

Speak, for your servant is listening

It is easy enough to pretend to ask God to speak while having no intention at all to listen. In their different ways, and from their very different emotional situations, Hannah, Eli and Samuel, all tried seriously to listen to what might be being said to them. The baton is being passed from the old to the young, and Samuel receives it well.

—12—

1 Samuel 16:7
(1 Samuel 16:1-13 for the context)

"The Lord looks
at the heart"

Samuel arrives in Bethlehem and is there to anoint a successor to King Saul. The relentless demand of the Israelites to have a king like other nations was being answered. Saul was the first king and at this point in the narrative is still officially in charge. But the tide is turning: he is not acting as a divinely-anointed king should be acting and it is increasingly clear that a new ruler will be needed at some point. In Bethlehem Samuel is tempted to follow his immediate response to what he sees in front of him as he looks at prospective candidates from the family of Jesse, grandson of Ruth and Boaz.

But he pauses, and a quiet voice reminds him that while outward appearances may matter to some people, it is what is inside that truly counts.

The Lord does not look at the things people look at. Human beings look at the outward appearance, but the Lord looks at the heart

Young David is called in from the fields and he is chosen, not his stronger, more experienced, older brothers. We are not told what was in David's heart which meant that he would fit this calling although his personality is inevitably increasingly revealed as the story unfolds. Perhaps it is not our business, it is what is in our heart, not our neighbour's that we should be most concerned about.

As the narrative continues it is clear that whatever is in David's heart, it is not perfection. He has the capacity for awful behaviour, as will be seen in his actions towards Bathsheba and Uriah. But there is a continuing, underlying desire to see God's name honoured among his people; there are many moments of courage, honour, compassion and integrity; he knows what it is to love; he knows what it is to say sorry when he gets it wrong.

The Lord looks at the heart

Samuel was briefly tempted to look for the outward signs of worldly achievements but was still alert to hearing from God, as he had been as a child. He had not become over-proud of his status or believed that his standing, experience and wisdom were all that he needed. He knew he had to stay listening.

For those who lack many worldly achievements it may be encouraging that the Lord looks at the heart. For those who take no trouble in checking whether the heart is in the right place, who do not think that love and truth matters but who are rather good at putting up a good front, then this is all rather unsettling.

Many centuries later Paul, who would have known this story by heart, urges a group of Christians in Corinth to remember that the choices we make in our hearts are the ones that truly matter. What we do and what we know may be important, but love matters much more.

"If I speak in human or angelic tongues, but have not love, I am only a resounding gong or a clanging cymbal. If I have the gift of prophecy and can fathom all mysteries and all knowledge, and if I have faith than can move mountains, but have not love, I am nothing, If I give all I possess to the poor and surrender my body to the flames, but have not love, I gain nothing."

The Lord looks at the heart

–13–

1 Samuel 17:39
(1 Samuel 17 for the context)

"I cannot go in these"

The anointing by Samuel has taken place but nothing then seems to happen. Sometime later, David, still a boy, is sent with sandwiches to his brothers who are preparing to battle the Philistines. While he is there he hears the taunts of Goliath. In his inexperience and naivety he does not understand why the Israelites do not respond. He has a row with his older brother Eliab who tells him that he is being pushy and annoying. King Saul hears what is going on, responds more gently and agrees that David can offer to fight Goliath; he even lends him his armour.

David walks around with various parts of the king's armour strapped around him and realises it is too big and heavy. He apologetically removes the armour and explains:

I cannot go in these

David knows he cannot dress up as someone else. Saul's armour does not fit and so, despite all the honour and protection it may carry, it is not for him. David instead relies on his experience and self-knowledge. He knows that he is good with the sling and that he does not scare easily; he knows that he needs to be able to move freely; he believes that God is with him. "The Lord who delivered me from the paw of the lion and the paw of the bear will deliver me from the hand of this Philistine."

He takes off the armour, picks up his sling, carefully chooses five suitable stones and approaches Goliath. Goliath laughs and jeers, and is perhaps angry that the Israelites, by sending out a boy instead of one of their champions, seem to be mocking him. But he is not concentrating and is forgetful of his military knowledge. A well-aimed slingshot can be deadly (ancient armies used slingers as well as archers). Too busy mocking to be alert, he is hit hard in a vulnerable spot on his skull and he falls.

I cannot go in these

The temptation to dress up as someone else can be powerful, especially if it will add to prestige amidst a circle of family and friends. To wear the king's armour is a great honour. But David knows who he is, is thankful for his story so far and offers himself as he is to the battle. No doubt willing to learn from others but free from the temptation to pretend to be them. He does not need to fight the battle in their way.

It would have taken courage to say to Saul, who had been gracious and generous, that now was not the time to receive this gift. But David's strong-mindedness is a feature of the narrative. It is he, not the more experienced and cautious soldiers, who feels that Goliath has crossed a line and must be challenged. It is he who is so passionate about the honour of his people and his God that he feels something must be done. It is he who wants to takes on Goliath.

No wonder his older brother found him embarrassing and irritating. It is unlikely that this would have bothered David very much.

—14—

2 Samuel 12:7
(2 Samuel 11:1- 2 Samuel 12:7 for the context)

"You are the man"

That took some courage.

David is now a great and popular ruler. His defeat of Goliath had raised his profile and after an uneasy and sometimes dangerous relationship with Saul he had become king and Saul was dead. The reign is going well. There is then an unexpected incident which seems to come from nowhere: He lusts after a married woman, Bathsheba, gets her pregnant, unsuccessfully tries to induce her husband to sleep with her so the adultery will not be suspected and then has the husband, a brave and loyal soldier called Uriah, killed to prevent the scandal becoming public. He has got away with having an affair, with deceit and with the killing of a good and trusted servant of the crown.

And in front of him now stands Nathan, who believes that God has told him that David has committed these crimes.

Nathan tells a story of theft and power.

David is suitably outraged and, full of righteous indignation, demands to know the name of the sinner.

"You are the man," says Nathan.

How will David react? In one of the best moments of his life he honours the truth that has been spoken to him. He does not call for the guards or the lawyers, he does not justify himself or reach for his sword. He does not rage or plot and kill again. He crumbles and confesses.

He goes on to write what is now called the 51st Psalm, a moving and inspirational song of sorrow, insight, repentance, faith and hope. And later he will allow this song to be published.

David had sinned through being in the wrong place (he should have been at war like the other kings), through staring in the wrong direction (if you see someone undressing, you look away), and through thinking the wrong thoughts (I can take Bathsheba and hide the fact from everyone else. I can lie to Uriah and if that does not work I will have him killed). In this season of temptation he thought that none of the normal rules applied to him. But they apply to all of us, even to kings.

We do not know if David is in some way relieved, or simply terrified, when Nathan reminds him that nothing is secret from God. We do not know how his conscience has been handling his adultery and murder. When Nathan speaks these words, David knows how deep he has fallen but knows he can be forgiven. He knows the awfulness of what he has done but knows that his God is a God of second chances. In Psalm 51 he writes "Cleanse me with hyssop, and I shall be clean; Wash me, and I shall be whiter than snow. Let me hear joy and gladness; let the bones you have crushed rejoice."

You are the man

It is not easy being a Nathan, but sometimes that is the calling.

It is not easy being on the receiving end of a Nathan conversation, but it is sometimes necessary. And how we react is very revealing.

—15—

1 Kings 3:9
(1 Kings 3:1-15 for the context)

"Give your servant a discerning heart"

Not wealth, palaces or victories.

In due time David dies and his son Solomon replaces him as king. In a dream, Solomon is asked by God what he truly wants. He asks for wisdom.

Give your servant a discerning heart

'The wisdom of Solomon' has become proverbial, but what Solomon asks for is interestingly specific: "Give your servant a discerning heart to govern your people and to distinguish between right and wrong." Solomon believes that the wisdom he needs is twofold: Good leadership of a large, diverse and strong-willed group of subjects and good judgement in making the right moral choices (is the sad example of his father David's immorality with Bathsheba on his mind?).

Cultures and societies have varied in the im-

55   *Chapter —15—*

portance they have placed on the concept of morality. In some contexts, reference points for moral choices are not discussed at all or stridently asserted without challenge or analysis. At other times the need for careful wisdom to discern the right decisions in difficult situations is taken appropriately seriously and much good thinking takes place.

The book of Proverbs, associated closely with Solomon, stresses the importance of wisdom, as do, more implicitly, the other 'wisdom' books – Psalms, Job, Ecclesiastes and the Song of Solomon. This wisdom is expressed in songs and poems, in stories and in musings, and it covers all aspects of a person's relationship to God and to neighbour.

Wisdom, much more important than cleverness, is offered to everyone, whatever the background. In the eighth chapter of the book of Proverbs wisdom is personified, and the link is made to good choosing and good speaking. Wisdom says: "I raise my voice to all humanity. You who are simple, gain prudence; you who are foolish, gain understanding. Listen, for I have worthy things to say; I open my lips to speak what is right. My mouth speaks what is true, for my lips detest wickedness. All of the words of my mouth are just, none of them is crooked or perverse."

Give your servant a discerning heart

Solomon asks for wisdom and is then immediately called to exercise the gift he has been given. The narrator takes us to a difficult judgement to be made regarding two women and a baby. This is not a matter of national importance, but wisdom is to be exercised in the street as well as the embassy; it is to be practised over the washing up as much as in the seminar room; it is for the crèche as much as the palace.

Solomon's prayer is one that anyone can use: seeking discernment to serve those around us well, discernment to make the right moral choices. It is not a bad way of starting a reign, or simply each new day.

And Solomon sees it as the most important prayer he can make.

—16—

1 Kings 12:14
(1 Kings12: 1-16 for the context)

"I will scourge you with scorpions"

An unpleasant phrase.

Rehoboam had succeeded his father Solomon as king. He has learned little from the wisdom of his father. That in itself is thought-provoking: wisdom is given, discovered, gained, prayed for, sought, modelled – but it is not automatically inherited.

He begins well, asking for advice from young and old as to how he should govern the country. The old advise caution and gentleness, suggesting that he wins the people with humility and patience. These are uncertain times for the kingdom, think carefully about what your role needs to be. The young tell him to be tough: Go in hard, scourge them with scorpions. Show them who's boss. Be noticeably stricter than your predecessor.

Rehoboam follows the advice of the young

men. He summons the representatives of the nation and tells them "I will scourge you with scorpions".

What follows is resentment and disaster, and the country is divided.

What is happening inside of a person when they make the decision to be vicious and oppressive to others? Is Rehoboam scared of what people might do if they are allowed to flourish as themselves? Does he have something to prove within himself or to himself? Perhaps he simply enjoys the power of causing hurt to others; some people do.

There is something important in this narrative about whose voices we listen to most closely. Perhaps Rehoboam thinks that the excitement of the young is better than the experience of the aged. Or that he could not face his contemporaries if he took a more mature line, but he could discount the importance of relationships with the older counsellors. The enthusiasm and energy of young people are great gifts, but there is nothing intrinsically insightful about being young. (Some societies value youthful appearance so much that they unconsciously rather strangely believe that unwrinkled skin is a sign of profound philosophical depth.) There is likewise nothing intrinsically wise in being old but there is likely to be experience that is worth hearing. And among those older counsellors there were some who indeed had turned experience into wisdom. Rehoboam chooses not to listen.

It can be tempting to use terror as a weapon but it can be a sign of laziness as well as insecurity. Perhaps Rehoboam was not bothered to look at the situation from the other person's point of view or even was scared to engage properly with them. Perhaps he was not prepared to engage with his own frustrations, and instead simply turned his anger to those whom he could oppress.

Like so many dictators, whether in an empire, nation, the work place or the home, Rehoboam fails to understands the strength of the resentment he is arousing in the oppressed.

And he forgets his place and responsibility in the big story. He is son of Solomon, grandson of David. He has no interest in his rich and humane heritage of which he should be part, he has no understanding of the value that God has put on his people, of whom Rehoboam is simply a steward.

Rehoboam disregarded the wisdom of the experienced, he believed he could control through cruelty, he forgot the value of those whom he was called to lead and he had no sense of pride in his heritage.

It was not a good combination.

—17—

1 Kings 19:4
(1 Kings 19 1-18 for the context)

"I have had enough, Lord"

It is a cry from the heart. And perhaps has echoes in many of us.

Elijah is one of the great figures in the Old Testament narrative. He stands up for the heritage, values and faith of a nation that is swiftly disintegrating. The divided kingdom that Rehoboam bequeathed was ruled by a succession of kings for the north and the south, some who remembered what the nation was meant to stand for, and rather a lot who sadly did not. Elijah and other prophets speak wise, reminding and challenging words to any who would listen (and, bravely, to some who would not). Elijah would come to be seen as the greatest prophet of all; in the New Testament, in the description of the great moment on the mount of transfiguration, it is Elijah who appears alongside Moses and Jesus.

In this episode, during the reign of Ahab. Elijah has just scored a notable victory over the prophets of Baal, it was perhaps his greatest moment. Queen Jezebel is very angry but that is only to be expected. But sometimes even expected pressures can be too much to face. Elijah collapses.

I have had enough, Lord

Elijah is given sleep and food, two of the essentials for a healthy recovery. He is reminded that he is not alone (despair can feel so isolating) and he is given a task.

He is not told that this low mood is a sign that he has failed (it is not). Rather he is gently, graciously, set on his feet again and his ministry continues. The narrator does not take Elijah's anguished cry out of the story, and indeed it is a noticeable theme in these ancient writings that unrelenting outward smiles are not a feature in the lives of the key characters.

I have had enough, Lord

Elijah receives the help given to him. He eats and sleeps as advised, he hears the truth that there are indeed seven thousand who are quietly on the same side and who have not bowed the knee to the false gods. He accepts the task of going back to talk to King Ahab one more time. He is given a reassuring succession plan, Elisha is to follow in his footsteps.

And he is granted a reminder of the still small voice of calm. That the power and voice of God may not always be found in the stormy and the spectacular, the earthquake, wind and fire, but in 'a gentle whisper.'

Elijah is strong enough to know he can say to God, "I have had enough," he does not need to pretend. And he is reminded that this is a God strong enough to be gentle. God has no need to shout, the whisper is enough. Elijah is on his way again.

May we be as honest in our feelings, and may we be as gentle with others in theirs.

—18—

"The king watched the hand as it wrote"

Understandably so.

The warnings of the prophets like Elijah had been ignored. The divided kingdoms had failed and were conquered and the people taken off into exile and captivity. The dream is over, earthly military power has had the final word. In the middle of a drunken feast, surrounded by goblets looted from the temple of the conquered Israelites, voices still ringing with smiling and meaningless praises to 'the gods of gold and silver, of bronze, iron, wood and stone,' King Belshazzar of Babylon can afford to be pleased with himself. He had invited a thousand nobles to the feast. He is the centre of it all, he can do what he wants.

And then the hand appears. And writes mystifying symbols on the wall.

The king watched the hand as it wrote

He watches it like a hawk. What is going on? Is there indeed a power greater than these lifeless items of gold and bronze? Belshazzar is no longer in control. He is not the most important being in the room, let alone the world, and inevitably, swiftly, there is the realisation of a higher accountability. Something or someone is watching Belshazzar and words are being written. Military conquest, plundering others and impressive, careless, parties do not have the final say after all.

Belshazzar regains some sense of authority. It is still his party. He wants to know what the hand has written. But none of his advisors and philosophers and priests can translate the words. In desperation he turns to Daniel, one of those despised, conquered, Israelites whose vision of God is so very different. Daniel had found favour with Nebuchadnezzar, Belshazzar's father, being a loyal and honest servant, and his abilities are remembered in this moment of panic.

The writing's on the wall. This is where the phrase comes from (although it is not used in this form in the narrative). Since Belshazzar's time the phrase has come to mean judgement and finality, but until Daniel arrives nobody can be sure if this is bad or good news. Although perhaps, just perhaps, Belshazzar and his guests had sensed that mocking the Jewish sacred vessels was at best rather tasteless and at worst a dangerous and reckless step.

The king watched the hand as it wrote

And now he humbly listens to this representative of the enfeebled Israelites. Daniel translates and does not shy away from saying difficult truths. He serves a higher power than any Babylonian king. He speaks plainly: Belshazzar's days have been numbered by God. He has been weighed in the scales and found wanting. His rule is over.

Perhaps as the story was told and re-told for generations people wondered what a divine hand would write if words were to be inscribed on walls of our rooms, halls and homes. Or on the walls of palaces and parliaments.

The narrative concludes in somewhat clinical fashion: "That very night, Belshazzar, king of the Babylonians, was slain, and Darius the Mede took over the kingdom, at the age of sixty-two."

And Darius's relationship with Daniel will give rise to one of the most famous stories of all.

—19—

Daniel 6:10
(Daniel 6 for the context)

"Where the windows
opened towards Jerusalem"

Darius is now in charge. Daniel and his fellow exiles are careful in how they stay true to their faith and values in the midst of a hostile society; they work hard and keep a low profile. But Daniel increasingly arouses the jealousy of government officials because his reliability and efficiency leads to him being the front-runner to be chief minister to the king, rather like Joseph had been to Pharaoh in Egypt all those years before.

Darius' own countrymen decide to trap Daniel by causing Darius to pass a law stating that for the next thirty days prayers could be offered only to the king, not to any other God. This was a law that Daniel could not obey, as they knew. If he took his faith and heritage seriously, he would pray. Then they would have him, it would be the lions' den for him.

Understanding all this, and guessing that this

was the end, Daniel went home, went upstairs to the room that opened towards Jerusalem and prayed three times a day. Visibly.

Where the windows opened towards Jerusalem

There is a mix of nostalgia, poignancy and courage in this phrase. Daniel is reminding himself of where his true home is. He is also making it clear to his enemies that he is not going to stop worshipping his God.

"How do we sing the Lord's song in a foreign land?" Daniel could well have had this question from Psalm 137 in his mind. What battles do I choose to fight? When do I risk my position or my life? When do I keep quiet and ignore the changes in values and spirituality that I seem to be faced with each day? I want to keep singing the song of my community and my God, but how do I sing it well? What compromises are needed?

Daniel decides that this is the moment when he will make a stand. It is not always easy to discern when it is right to do so, which event or statement means that now we must risk everything and calmly make clear that we go thus far but no further.

Daniel is not offensive or condemnatory. He simply quietly acts in the way that he feels is right.

He is duly arrested and thrown to the lions.

He survives the lions and Darius ponders

more deeply. He senses that Daniel is an innocent man. In a similar way to Pilate's later reaction to Jesus, Darius hesitates. Unlike Pilate, he follows through the logic of his thinking. Daniel is released and honoured, his jealous accusers are punished.

The effects on others of a person acting with integrity and grace are incalculable, whether miniscule or life-changing it is impossible to know. But whatever was going to happen to Daniel, as he decided to pray where the windows opened towards Jerusalem he knew he was being true to himself, his heritage, his community and his God.

And there is always power in that, whoever might be watching and whatever it might lead to.

—20—

Nehemiah 6:3
(Nehemiah 1 and onwards for the context)

"I am carrying on a great project and cannot go down"

Nehemiah, in exile, had felt called to rebuild the ruined temple back in Jerusalem in his homeland. Everything had fallen into place. He had been given permission by king Artaxerxes to go, support was forthcoming and materials were provided. There was opposition, but the building continued.

The opposition swings from mockery to temptation —'Your wall is rubbish and a fox could knock it down' to 'Come and join us for a pleasant chat on the plains, we are all reasonable people, why spend your time building unnecessary protection to guard your people and your faith? What is so important about your belief that you have to work so hard to defend it?'

I am carrying on a great project and cannot go

down

Nehemiah wants to stay and see the work through. He is not being confused or frightened by the opposition, he is not being worn down by tiredness, boredom or pressure. It may have been tempting to feel that he has done his bit, played his part. Surely no one can blame him if he lays down his trowel and goes to have a sensible discussion on the plains.

And so tasks are left half-finished. And so people strive for variety for its own sake rather than seeing something through. And so people walk away from relationships which once seemed so committed. People are tempted to write impressive variety into their career description, rather than seeing a role through.

Discerning when it is right to move and when it is right to stay is seldom an easy choice, especially when there are voices on both sides of the debate. It is not always clear when our part in a script is complete, when it is time to leave the stage to another. Living in a hurried society means that there are particular temptations to move too soon. Sometimes we are called to stay on the stage.

Nehemiah had become involved in the rebuilding after he had heard of the run-down state of Jerusalem. He was relatively comfortable in exile, with a good job, cupbearer to the king. He could have ignored the news and said it was not his problem. But his care for his people was so strong that he wept and prayed and acted. In his response he identifies himself with his old countrymen. In his words he becomes one of them, not simply watching from a distance.

He travels to Jerusalem, with authorisation from the king Artaxerxes. He plans carefully what is needed and then builds a large and effective team. The narrative of Nehemiah is full of names, he values the craftsmen and colleagues as individuals, not simply as faceless labourers. Spiritual reconstruction for his people is likewise a priority. The old books of the law are found and read publicly once again. They are moved by how much they have forgotten and begin to weep, but Nehemiah wants celebration and generosity: "Go and enjoy choice food and sweet drinks, and send some to those who have nothing prepared. This day is sacred to our Lord. Do not grieve, for the joy of the Lord is your strength."

Through it all Nehemiah had been on the receiving end of constant taunts and enmity from some, especially from Sanballat and Tobiah. Such voices can be wearing and tempting. Nehemiah is faithful to the task set before him. He knows its value, and knows it is not yet complete. He stays.

I am carrying on a great project and cannot go down

–21–

Luke 1:38
(Luke 1:26-38 for the context)

"May it be to me as

you have said"

We move to a new era. Many centuries have passed since Nehemiah stood firm on his wall. The people of Israel are back in their land but the Romans are now in control. The faithful continue to try and live as they feel called to do, but they are despised and oppressed; the ancient hopes and prophecies of a saviour figure seem increasingly ridiculous and irrelevant.

And then a teenage Jewish girl is visited by an angel.

May it be to me as you have said, she replies.

Some would have wanted to be more conditional. Some would have wanted to bargain with God, to gain something in return for this scandal, burden and unspeakable honour that were now being set in train.

But at this supreme moment in history Mary simply wants things to happen as God wants

73   *Chapter —21—*

them to happen. She has just been told that she, still a virgin, has become pregnant, that the baby is significant beyond all imagining, and that God himself somehow has been at work in the conception. She would have known how all this was going to sound to her fiancé Joseph, to her family and to her friends. What ridicule, contempt and pain lie ahead? She has little choice, but she does not complain or rant.

May it be to me as you have said

Whatever the cost will be, Mary accepts.

Mary visits her elderly cousin Elizabeth, who is also pregnant. That meeting brings comfort and reassurance. A few months later the baby is born, no doubt bringing much joy and relief, especially after the final worried search for accommodation in over-crowded Bethlehem. Shepherds unexpectedly arrive to pay homage and then, six miles back north in Jerusalem for the ritual presentation of a new baby in the temple, hope-filled words are said about Jesus. But Mary is also told by Simeon that 'a sword will pierce your soul.' All parenting is complex and piercing, but these would have been sad and strange words to hear spoken aloud in the midst of the joyful presentation and welcome. Back to Bethlehem and sometime later Magi appear, with gold, frankincense and myrrh. Gold for kingship, frankincense for priesthood, but myrrh is the spice for burial; the uneasy theme of mixed joy and sorrow is being continued. Then life as refugees, on the run from Herod until he dies, and finally ending up back in Nazareth. Losing twelve year old Jesus in the Temple (Joseph is not mentioned after this incident – did he die when Jesus was a teenager?). Mary, by now a widow, is named as being present at several points in Jesus' ministry and is at the foot of the cross watching her son die. A sword will pierce your soul. May it to be as you have said. Perhaps these words echoed round Mary's heart on that terrible Friday. And in the midst of being crucified, Jesus found breath to arrange for his friend John to look after Mary once he is gone.

And then Sunday happens, and the long-stored myrrh is not needed after all…

May it be to me as you have said

It is one of the biggest prayers in history. It contains power, promise and change that Roman Emperor Augustus, planning his census which would mean that Mary would be travelling to Bethlehem to have her baby, could not have foreseen, and neither did anyone else.

—22—

(Matthew 1:18-25 for the context)

"(He) did not want
to expose her to
public disgrace"

Joseph has just found out that his fiancée was pregnant. And he is not the father.

This was emotionally and socially devastating in Nazareth in those days, as it would be in many parts of the world today.

He pulls himself together and makes the decision to continue to treat Mary with respect and affection. He does not want to humiliate, he will treat her well.

Bethlehem, small and unimportant (but deeply historic – home of Ruth and then of David) had been promised a key role by the prophet Micah "But you, Bethlehem, Ephrathah, though you are small among the clans of Judah, out of you will come for me one who will be the ruler over Israel, whose origins are from old, from ancient times."

The birth of the messiah, a saviour figure, fits into the long story, and it is expected to happen in Bethlehem. Joseph, who at this point does not know that his story is to be part of this much bigger story, chooses to act with honour and compassion and the effects are immensely significant.

Perhaps they always are. Think of the relationships that would be saved or improved, the healings that could occur, the halting of spiralling down into private and public bitterness, if Joseph's example were followed more often. 'Whatever is happening, I am not going to disgrace this person.'

It is only after he decides on this course of action, that Joseph hears the angel explaining why it will be right to stay with Mary and he is told that these events will bring blessing to countless others. The order of these steps is significant: Joseph does not receive the confirmation until *after* he has chosen the honourable path. If Joseph had not stayed with Mary, then she would not have had to travel to Bethlehem (it was Joseph who was of David's line, not Mary) and the baby would have been born elsewhere.

His journey will not be an easy one. In staying faithful to Mary and his son, Joseph no doubt faced knowing glances or ridicule from friends and family. He then endured being forced to flee far from his home, no doubt doing all he could to provide for his family, perhaps selling his carpentry skills in Egyptian villages. Through all of Jesus' childhood – especially brought home by the events of the few days in the temple aged twelve – Joseph knows that he is not in full control of events in his family. This is a common enough feeling for parents, but especially so in Joseph's case, the ability be a *humble* father is a great gift.

We do not know if Joseph's death, when Jesus was still relatively young, was sudden or expected. As he died, perhaps he was comforted by the knowledge that in making the decision to act kindly towards Mary at a crucial and unsettling moment, he did right.

(He) did not want to expose her to public disgrace

Compassion, honour and kindness are never wasted.

—23—

"So that I too may go and worship him"

He lies.

Herod has no desire to worship the baby in Bethlehem. He wants to kill him. Jesus is a threat, born into the blood line of the great King David, born in David's town. King Herod is not a real king at all, he does not have royal blood running through his veins. The Romans allow him a measure of local power because he is good at control, but in his insecurity and fear he is capable of deceit and cruelty.

Why do people lie? What fears or manipulations play into our minds so that lies can spring so readily? Perhaps we want to please and impress. Perhaps we fear someone might take our place if we do not live up to the role we think is ours by right. Perhaps we want to stay king of our own little world and become oversensitive to any perceived threat.

As soon as you find him, report to me, so that I too may go and worship him

This is what he says to the Magi, as they search for the new baby. Herod is the only person in the Christmas narratives who lies and who does not 'go'. Herod has no interest in finding out what all this fuss around this birth might mean. His mind is closed, perhaps for the same reason that he lies. Truth is always dangerous.

The themes of truth and deceit, hypocrisy and openness, frequently reappear in Jesus' life and teaching. When Pontius Pilate, Roman Governor, speaks to Jesus on that later Friday morning in Jerusalem, he asks the question "What is truth?" But he does not wait for an answer, preferring instead to go out to the crowd.

In some ways Herod is right. He, politically very skilful, adept at handling the Roman occupiers, senses that something potentially significant is happening here in Bethlehem. What he misunderstands is that the challenge is not to him as an earthly king, but to him as a person. This Jesus is not going to want to take his crown, he is going to want to change his life. And this can be much more unsettling. Whether for political or personal reasons, Herod reaches for the sword.

Herod wanted to be remembered, he wanted to leave a legacy that would be talked about for centuries, and hence he invested in spectacular buildings. He did not realise that his character, his deceit and his cruelty, would be remembered much more widely than his architecture.

As soon as you find him, report to me, so that I too may go and worship him

The Magi do not believe him, once they find the baby they do not send word to Herod. Herod is powerful but is not trustworthy. The Magi recognise that, as the wise always do.

—24—

Luke 2:10
(Luke 2:1-20 for the context)

"Good news of great joy that will be for all the people"

Before the Magi arrive, before Herod begins to worry, shepherds are doing what they usually do in the fields outside Bethlehem. An ordinary job in ordinary times in an ordinary place. And then angels appear. Modern readers will want to know what these angels looked like, so would have Theophilus, who first received this account from Luke. Luke does not go into detail. He is tantalisingly and impressively silent, as he was when describing the angelic visitation to Mary. This is what eye-witnesses have told me, I need say no more.

Good news of great joy that will be for all the people

This is the message of the angels to the shepherds describing the birth of Jesus.

The bar is being set very high – this news is good, it contains joy, it is for all people.

What is meant by 'good'? Is there something here about news that is honest and constructive, news that will change things for the better? Is there something about holiness?

What brings joy? Is there something here about love, reconciliation, healing, satisfaction, hope and purpose?

For all the people? If this is good news of great joy for everyone, then here is something that can reach every person on the planet. Every person, of all ages, backgrounds, cultures and creeds. This is not about a tribal religion, this is extensive and inclusive.

This then is news that makes a difference, news that is likely to be about love and news that values each person seriously, not necessarily affirming where they are, but always affirming what they can be. The angels go on to say that "a saviour has been born", underlining that the good news of great joy for all people is to be a saving ministry of rescuing, reconciling, forgiving, restoring relationships, with God and with others. But the title 'saviour' only makes sense if I accept I need saving. Perhaps this news includes challenge as well as comfort.

Do the shepherds want to hear the news? Won't we look rather silly turning up at a stable and saying that angels told us to come and look at a baby? Why do they think we need to be saved? Who are these angels anyway? Isn't the whole concept of sin rather outdated? If this 'good news' is about love, then love always involves choice to say no as well as yes. Perhaps we are not the sort of people who like to ask for help… There were all sorts of reasons why it might have felt safer to stay out in the fields.

Today in the town of David a Saviour has been born to you.

The shepherds would have noticed that Bethlehem is not called 'Bethlehem' by the angels; they would have understood the significance of 'town of David'. There is something in this birth which will have an echo of David, the great shepherd king. They, shepherds, have been chosen to hear the news, perhaps this baby will indeed be the shepherd of his people, or is there something here about lambs, and their ancient role as being sacrificial offerings?

And they may have wondered if the theme of David as conquering hero is to be repeated, not yet knowing that what needed to be conquered was something rather bigger than the forces of the Roman Empire.

They would not have known that this baby would grow up to say "I am the good shepherd," but they would have known that David had written a Psalm which began "The Lord is my shepherd." They are shepherds too, they make up their minds; it seems worth the short journey into Bethlehem to find out more, and so they go.

—25—

Matthew 14:8
(Matthew 14:1-13 for the context)

"Give me the head of
John the Baptist"

It is thirty or so years later and an evening of drunkenness, spite, pride, showing off and rash promises draws towards an end.

Relationships between a young woman and her step-father can be complex. Herod (the son of the Herod mentioned in the Bethlehem narratives) perhaps wants Salome (probably her name but we cannot be certain) to like him, or is confused or entranced by the dance, or wants to be seen as the one in charge, to be the big man of the evening. He promises the world. His wife, and the girl's mother, Herodias, is not interested in the world or what her daughter might want. This is not the moment for a golden cup from the table, jewels or a new palace. Herodias, ice-cold, wants revenge on the man who had highlighted her moral failings. Nothing else matters.

Give me the head of John the Baptist

This I Call to Mind   86

On a plate, so we can laugh at it as being fitting for a feast.

The mood changes. The guests wonder how their host will react. A better man would have dismissed such a suggestion with a laugh or a sharp word, but the pressure of a social situation can be powerful. Herod feels trapped (in truth he is not) and orders the execution.

Does he truly think this will cause Herodias, her daughter and the guests to like and respect him?

The order is given with a heavy heart. Yes, John is a challenging man but there is something about him that grabs attention, something that speaks of deep integrity, someone worth listening to. And Herod is having him killed. Because he was showing off in front of his friends, because he had drunk too much, because he wanted to impress a young girl, because he was behaving like a silly old man. And now he will live with the realisation that others think he is exactly that.

Bring me the head of John the Baptist. The one who had called Israel to repentance, who had baptised and welcomed, who had recalled in people's minds the great prophets of the past, who had opened a new chapter in the history of Israel, and who had talked about a coming messiah. An exhilarating and dynamic figure. A breath of fresh air.

And now messily decapitated in a dungeon

because Herod has handled a party particularly badly.

It is a sad story. So much harm is so often done from grubby, sordid, beginnings.

Did Herod sleep well that night?

Did Herodias?

Did Salome?

When Jesus heard what had happened he went to find a solitary place. Perhaps he wept for his cousin John. Perhaps he wept for Herod, for Herodias, and for Salome. Perhaps he wept for those of us for whom this story has uneasy echoes. And for a world where such things can happen.

—26—

Luke 5:20
(Luke 5:17-26 for the context)

"Friend, your sins are forgiven"

They were not expecting that.

After the death of John the Baptist Jesus continues to teach and proclaim that 'the Kingdom of God is near'. There seem to be deep riches and power in what he is doing and saying; it is not always easy but increasingly intriguing to try and put a finger on what is causing his magnetism.

The paralysed man had been lowered through the roof into the house where Jesus was speaking. The little house was already so packed with people that no-one could not get through the door. The friends become inventive and come through the ceiling, (their committed friendship is an inspiration in itself, aside from the importance of what is about to happen). Once they finally get him in the room they hope for a physical healing, it is difficult to imagine anything more helpful and exciting than that. But instead they hear Jesus say:

Friend, your sins are forgiven

What does the preacher know about this man that causes him to say that? Why does he think he has the authority to declare that his sins are forgiven? Why does he say this before he comments on the physical paralysis?

Because sins matter. They spoil relationships, contentment and potential. They separate people from God. They cause a wallowing in darkness rather than enjoying the light. They weigh people down with guilt and regret. And Jesus is making the outrageous claim that he can forgive them.

Friend, your sins are forgiven

Jesus will go on to heal the person physically, but wants to make the point that spiritual healing is always the priority. He is assuming the authority to use the God-words of forgiveness, and this is completely shocking. Who does he think he is?

Later, Paul, who was very self-aware of his own sin and spiritual and emotional struggles, was to write with absolute confidence in his letter to the Romans: "There is now no condemnation for those who are in Christ." No condemnation. None at all. The slate wiped clean, the new day dawning. Guilt taken away.

Peter, who was equally honest about his own failings, was to write about Jesus: "He himself bore our sins in his body on the tree, so that we might die to sin and live for righteousness; by his wounds you have been healed."

All these weighty words are for the future. In the packed house the immediate effect on the person, his friends and those watching, was one of shock. Everything has been moved to a different sphere. The physical healing that follows then seems an added extra, supporting the main event of the spiritual restoration.

And perhaps some would remember that the first word that Jesus says to the person is 'friend'.

Chapter —26

—27—

"Some fell along the path"

Story-telling was Jesus' favoured way of teaching, as it was to many Jewish rabbis then and since. A story is often more accessible and memorable than a didactic approach.

Jesus is telling a story about a farmer and talks about the need for fertile soil if the seed is to flourish.

A farmer went out to sow his seed. As he was scattering the seed, some fell along the path

The opening of the story would have caused knowing glances among the listeners and perhaps a sneer or two. The path is not a good place to sow seed.

The farmer is wasteful and careless. He is not targeting his sowing of the seed, he is throwing it anywhere and everywhere. It is obvious that he has not been to the right farming college or attended the right strategy courses, his professional development seems to have gone rather astray. He simply scatters the seed. And the story continues this theme, as well as on the path, some is flung into rocky soil, some among thistles. The wasteful approach would have caused raised eye-brows among the knowledgeable agricultural community of first century Judea.

But this, Jesus is saying, is how God works. His love will constantly be offered everywhere. Much seed will be ignored or be easily crushed or fail to take deep roots. But the seed will be thrown. Wasteful, extravagant indeed.

But one never knows...

Perhaps the farmer knows better than the listeners. Perhaps what the listeners consider to be paths and thistles are more fertile than they realise. Conversely, perhaps there are hidden, defensive, rocks beneath what looks to be fertile earth. From a distance it is hard to know what is shallow or deep soil.

The listeners' responsibility is to examine their own hearts, to consider where they would be in the story. Are they willing to allow the seed go deep? Is it always easy to see how strong one's own thistles of stress and pressure might be, or what hidden resistance there might be to unconditional, relentless, love? Can they see the large rocks of selfishness or pride which mean it is a struggle for the baby plant to find purchase with its fragile roots? But amidst the challenging questions there is the encouragement: if the soil is right then the harvest will be great indeed.

Chapter —27—

Those who follow Christ are similarly called to be extravagant in sowing the love of God, scattering it far and wide, being faithful in generosity in sharing the good news in word and action. Throughout history, and perhaps in our own lives, there have been unexpectedly large and fruitful plants from very scanty beginnings.

At some point seed of the news of God's love was scattered in our direction. It is good to be thankful for those who were faithful in following the example of the divine sower.

—28—

Luke 10:37
(Luke 10:25-37 for the context)

"Go and do likewise"

As simple as that.

Jesus' story of the Samaritan who helps when those who should, don't, was told in response to the question "Who is my neighbour?" This question carried many religious, cultural, political and philosophical undercurrents. It was as old as Cain's "Am I my brother's keeper?", as contemporary as attitudes towards the occupying Romans and as emotive as the centuries-old hatred between the Jews and the Samaritans. Jesus tells a story which touches on some of the underlying issues, but the parting shot is unashamedly practical. It is not 'let's have another seminar on this sometime', it is *Go and do likewise*.

It is as if Jesus is saying: Enough of the philosophical discussion, although do remember the message about rethinking your expectations of people whom you despise, such as the Samaritans. Enough of the pondering of why the supposedly good people pass by on the other side, challenging and important though that is. Enough of the asking of the questions to see if Jesus can be trapped in a clever conversation, however stimulating these robust engagements always are. Please, a little less conversation, a little more action.

Jesus is always practical. Whatever the listeners may feel about what they are learning, they are expected to act. Attitudes and behaviours are expected to change.

In another story, perhaps one of the most unsettling he tells, Jesus makes the claim that "Whatever you did for one of the least of these brothers and sisters of mine, you did for me". A contrast is made with those who do not help the needy; they are told "Whatever you did not do for one of the least of these, you did not do for me."

The theological claim is enormous: Jesus is present in my neighbour. What does that say about Jesus and what does it say about my neighbour? The practical and emotional implications are equally large. Every act of kindness matters because it is being offered to Jesus as it is being offered to the neighbour. Nothing will be wasted or forgotten because the mind of God encompasses and remembers all.

And every act of unkindness matters, too. No wonder quite a number of people thought it would be easier if Jesus were to die. Part of the fear of Jesus, the running away from the challenge, was because of the tendency to take Jesus' stories in isolation from each other. To remember only the challenging and not the comforting – there is an equal danger in remembering only the comforting. Jesus' parables contain a rich mix of mercy as well as challenge. God loves people so much that forgiveness is constantly on offer, but the love includes the highest of aspirations and expectations for us. He wants the best for us, he challenges us. But he understands that we often fail. And when we fail, he will always pick us up.

Go and do likewise

But there are more urgent and pressing calls on my time, so many reasons why I should pass by on the other side.

Go and do likewise

—29—

Luke 15:20
(Luke 15: 11-32 for the context)

"He ran to his son"

Jesus must have been joking, they would have said. This particular story has now become a pantomime.

But he is not joking; the story is a serious one and one of the most significant that Jesus tells. Yes, the old man really does run. But the listeners knew that men, in those days, do not run. It was undignified, not in accordance with their status and venerability. Not what was expected.

The father runs, so excited to see his child come back that he throws dignity to the winds. He has been waiting and watching for this moment. The love counts more than other people's expectations. The love counts more than the servants' disbelieving stares as they see their master clutching his robes untidily and sprinting down the path.

He ran to his son

The son was not coming back in triumph. This was not a welcome back to someone who

This I Call to Mind

98

had done the family proud and who was full of memories of applause and success. This was someone who had made unkind and disastrous choices and who had dragged his name (and his family's name) into the mud. He had taken half of his father's wealth, too impatient to wait until the old man had died. He had wasted and lost it in a sordid and unsatisfying lifestyle. No wonder he was coming back with head held low and wondering if there was space for him somewhere in the servants' quarters.

He ran to his son

And embraces him, and brings him home. Gives him the best robe, sacrifices the prize fatted-calf and throws a party.

But the journeying is not finished. The father goes out again, this time to the discourteous older brother (it was a serious and significant social slur for an oldest son not to attend his father's party). Although his resentment is understandable, the older brother does not seem to understand how this family works. Why wasn't he running with his father to meet his long-lost younger brother? That really would have given the servants something to think about. But perhaps long-festering bitterness has swallowed up affection. The father does not scold, he responds to the older son with patience and asks him to open his eyes to all that he is given.

The younger son had the sense to come

home. Whatever rebuke he feared might await him, he knew that home was safe. But there is no rebuke, there is no 'I told you so'. There is no 'let's see how it goes for a few weeks'. None of that is needed because the child has decided to come home. "He came to his senses" is how Jesus describes that repentance moment, that turning back from the shame and the waste to return to the spiritual and emotional place where he truly belongs. The concept of true 'home' is very strong in the scriptures, and Jesus is deliberately using this evocative image in this story.

The father ran to his child. That is what he does, every time. And welcomes home.

—30—

"One of them, when he saw
he was healed, came back"

Jesus is travelling in the tense borderlands between Samaria and Galilee. Ten people suffering from leprosy see him and, from a distance, ask to be healed. Jesus does so, simply by telling them to perform the duty of going to the priest for confirmation that the disease is gone. They obey, and they are healed.

One of them, when he saw he was healed, came back

He comes back, throws himself at Jesus' feet, and thanks him. Jesus accepts the thanks: "Rise and go, your faith has made you well." It seems that something deeper is going on; all ten had been healed physically, but in the coming back and the thanking, this one had been healed in a different way.

He came back.

It would have been understandable that in the

excitement of the healing he did not give time to come back. With less dramatic blessings it is even easier to forget what has gone well, or to take the trouble to be thankful.

It is easy to feel too busy to spend a few moments at the end of each day reflecting on the good things, going back to those moments of answered prayer and being thankful for them. Or perhaps the temptation is to think that God had no part in it at all, that the success was due entirely to our own efforts and there is no need to be thankful. Or perhaps we simply shift our anxiety onto something else and we are too preoccupied to be thankful for the solution to the previous object of our worry.

Jesus notes wryly that the one who comes back with thanksgiving and humility is one of the despised Samaritans. This episode is typical of one of the ongoing themes in his ministry. Those who should have recognised the long-awaited messiah, did not. Perhaps they had different expectations, perhaps they did not want the challenge. But others did, especially the outcasts.

(Mediaeval artists caught this theme when they included the ox and the ass in their paintings of the nativity. The gospel writers do not mention them being present but there was an old prophecy in the first chapter of Isaiah: "The ox knows its master, the donkey its owner's manger, but Israel does not know, my people do not understand." The painters are smilingly reminding us that perhaps even the animals can see when something special is going on, but those who think they are seeing clearly often miss it.)

The hero of this narrative understands the emotional and spiritual importance of taking time to come back in heart and mind (and sometimes physically) to the place of blessing, and to say thank you. And in doing so a new chapter is opened for him.

—31—

John 8:6
(John 8:1-11)

"(He) started to write
on the ground"

We do not know what he wrote. Or whether the woman or accusers were able to see what he was writing.

The woman had been caught in adultery and dragged in front of Jesus. There is no sign of the man, which raises its own questions about the justice of the event, and it is quickly clear that the morality or otherwise of adultery is not the primary concern of the accusers. They are the establishment, Pharisees and the teachers of the Law, and their primary aim to trap Jesus. Will he uphold the letter of the Law and endorse the stoning of the woman, or will he refuse to do so? Whose side is he on?

Jesus crouches down and writes on the ground. He pauses and then looks up: "Let any of you who is without sin be the first to throw a stone at her."

This I Call to Mind   104

There must have been something piercing about the way Jesus spoke. No one in the crowd steps forward to say "Well I may not be perfect but at least I have not done that" or "What about the Law?" They are silent, turn one by one, and leave. The older ones first. Perhaps with more years to reflect upon, they are more vividly aware of their own sins and the times when they have been shown mercy by others. After all their mistakes and sins, why now destroy this woman?

Only Jesus and the woman are left. He does not condemn her either, but neither does he overlook the sin. He tells her it is time for a new chapter.

The Pharisees and the teachers of the Law would have been frustrated. It is not impossible that they set up the whole event (why was the man not brought?) in order to trap Jesus into a fatal explicit rejection of the Law. But Jesus is skilful at avoiding such traps, as equally shown by his answer to the question on another occasion as to whether it was right to pay taxes to the Romans. Jesus is in control of his timetable. When it is time for him to die, then he will accept the betrayal and the arrest; until then he will not allow others to set the agenda

The accusers had come filled of self-righteousness indignation, but they left with their own consciences and memories stirred. Jesus does tend to make things personal, often simply by asking questions.

The woman would have been terrified but Jesus brings peace. Whatever others may say, whatever harm they may cause us, Jesus treats us with compassion and with purpose.

We do not know what he wrote on the ground. Perhaps he was playing for time or quoting appropriate ancient texts. Perhaps he was simply distressed by their lack of sympathy or wanted to show that writing in the sand is temporary but a person's life is bigger. We do not know. Whatever it was it provided a pause. And in that pause perhaps people's minds began to turn to kinder rhythms.

In their haste to hear the voice of Jesus they learned that he will not be rushed for quick answers. If he wants to doodle in the sand, then so he will. And it may be a pause that is worth hearing.

—32—

Luke 19:5
(Luke 19:1-10 for the context)

"Zacchaeus"

Jesus knew his name. Perhaps he had been told who it was who was in the tree. Perhaps he simply knew. Perhaps he asked.

There is something powerful about names. They remind us of identity, individuality and difference, that we are more than statistics. Zacchaeus and the others in Jericho that day would have known the ancient verse from the prophet Isaiah, in which God says "I have summoned you *by name*; you are mine."

When Zacchaeus woke up that morning and heard the news that the preacher from the north was travelling through Jericho on his way to Jerusalem he would have had a mix of emotions. As a tax-collector, paying commission to the occupying Romans, he would have been feared, despised and ignored. He understandably does not want to mingle with the crowd who are turning out to see this controversial, comforting and unsettling preacher. But he wants to see

Jesus.

He climbs a tree so he can look from a safe distance. And then he hears the voice calling:

Zacchaeus

He is not expecting that. And it is followed up by something equally important, Jesus invites himself to Zacchaeus' house. Receiving and giving hospitality was as significant then as it is now, Zacchaeus knows that this is an honour, "He came down at once and welcomed him gladly."

Others equally know the significance and react angrily – "He has gone to be the guest of a sinner." Why can't Jesus ever get it right?

Jesus goes to Zacchaeus' house. We are not told what happens in the conversation but can assume that it was about more than the weather, Jesus has a habit of liking to go deep.

Zacchaeus emerges and something has changed, he will give recompense to those he has cheated. But he is not simply moving from reverse to neutral, he wants to move from reverse to forward, and thus wants also to give half his possessions to the poor. He may be a relatively rich man but this is still a serious, sacrificial, charitable commitment.

Zacchaeus

Jesus knows people by name, and he knows what needs to be said in private conversations.

There is no one outside his interest and care,

not even tax-collecting, Roman-serving, greedy businessmen.

Luke seems particularly interested in this brief visit to Jericho. He records an incident just before Jesus reaches the town when he is approached by a blind beggar. As with Zacchaeus, others had wanted to quieten down this encounter. As with Zacchaeus, Jesus ignores the muttering. He always does.

Jesus is going through Jericho because he is journeying to Jerusalem. To the week that will change history. But he has time for tea with Zacchaeus on the way.

—33—

John 12:3
(John 12:1-8 for the context)

"And the house was filled with the fragrance of the perfume"

It was all rather embarrassing. Everyone was probably slightly on edge anyway, this being the Saturday just before the week of the great festival of Passover. Jesus is outside Jerusalem, in Bethany on the Mount of Olives. The city itself is filling up. From across the Mediterranean world worshippers are travelling towards this great feast of sacrifice and liberation.

His friends had sensed that Jesus' arrival at the feast is going to be particularly significant this year. There has been an intentionality in the way he has been 'setting his face' towards Jerusalem. And rather strange comments about suffering, dying and rising.

Martha is doing what she does so well. Serving faithfully and usefully. We know that sometimes

This I Call to Mind

110

she is so committed to doing things that she forgets sometimes simply to sit down with Jesus.

And Lazarus is there, brought back from the dead by Jesus, sitting there, probably wondering somewhat what is going on.

And, according to John, Mary (sister of Lazarus, not the mother of Jesus) unties her hair, which was a socially shocking action in those days, and pours expensive perfume all over Jesus' feet.

And the house was filled with the fragrance of the perfume

It is an extravagant and generous gesture. Judas, either severely practical or very grumpy (it is sometimes not easy to differentiate between the two), points out the financial cost of all this. Jesus responds with an extraordinary statement that what is about to happen to him in Jerusalem will ultimately encompass the needs of the whole world, and that Judas need not be quite so concerned.

Mary is whole-hearted in her service of Jesus. She is humble in anointing the feet, not the head. Others do not understand.

But Jesus does, and accepts her attempt to show her love for him.

And perhaps Mary and others present later pondered his response, and were reminded that generosity has its own value, has significance beyond our understanding and that it is always well received. And that Jesus knew he was coming to Jerusalem to die. This is the anointing before his burial.

Mary's whole-heartedness, humility and acceptance of being misunderstood, are powerful qualities that speak of deep love.

No wonder that the house was filled with the fragrance of the perfume.

—34—

"Our lamps are going out"

And this, in the context of this story, is a problem. Jesus is painting a scene in which ten young women, due to be part of a wedding feast, are waiting to accompany the bridegroom to the festivities. They do not know exactly when he will appear, but know they must keep their oil lamps replenished in readiness for his arrival.

Five do so, no doubt checking often that the oil level is high enough. Five do not and one by one their lamps flicker and die.

The five 'foolish' ones ask the five 'wise' ones for oil, but it is noted that no-one will then have enough; the point being made here is not about selfishness but about being resourced ourselves, we cannot rely on others' spiritual vitality.

Perhaps the foolish had thought that one experience was all that was needed. I have the memory, I have the certificate, I was at that event, surely that will see me through.

It is Passover week and Jesus is acting and

teaching powerfully among the crowds in Jerusalem. He has turned over tables, physically and metaphorically, challenging directly about usefulness, fruitfulness and accountability. It is all rather uncomfortable. He keeps on telling pointed stories. This is one of them.

Our lamps are going out

In the Bible oil is often portrayed as a sign of the Holy Spirit, a sign of God's presence and blessing in a person's life. In Psalm 23 the divine shepherd 'anoints my head with oil'. As well as a sign of honour, anointing is a sign of closeness. You cannot anoint from a distance; you cannot fill oil lamps from a distance. The blessing of a relationship with God is an intimate one.

To be ready for the bridegroom's return the lamps have to be replenished. "Keep in step with the Spirit" writes Paul to the Galatians, using the image of a shared journey rather than oil. The relationship has to be maintained.

What might Jesus mean by keeping the oil replenished, what might Paul mean by keeping in step? There will be something here about love, faith, obedience, learning and fellowship, something about prayer, something about baptism and communion, something about compassion, forgiveness and the Bible. Many books have been written on this and many sermons preached, but perhaps the key points in Jesus' story are the *willingness* to stay replenished and the understanding that patience means keeping alert, not letting things slide.

In first-century lamps you cannot see the level of the oil from the outside. It does not matter how decorated or successfully shiny the surface may be. As with David being chosen to be king, it is what is on the inside that counts. The scruffiest, most chipped, lamps may be the ones that give the best light, if the oil is at a good level.

The wise took pains to be ready for the bridegroom. The foolish took their invitation for granted. Like any relationship, this one needs to be taken seriously.

—35—

"So they counted out for him thirty silver coins"

Judas, who had heard so many powerful words from Jesus about the dangers of the love of money, decided that these words were wrong and that money was to be treasured more than the life of the teacher.

As far as we know (and many have guessed) he does not betray his teacher and friend of three years for some vision of the greater good. Just for money. Thirty silver coins. We could look up how much that would be worth in today's money, but that is to miss the point. This is a moment of principle not price, and Judas chooses money. At that moment, in that context, the thing that matters most to Judas is the bag of coins, carefully counted out in front of him. Another day he may choose differently, but there was perhaps a deeper vulnerability in him that could be exploited in that moment of stress in the frenetic atmosphere of Passover week. Money can, for some, appear to mean stability, and Judas reaches for it.

Jesus had come in on the Sunday and had been hailed as king, "Hosanna to The Son of David" they had cried. He had not hushed the crowds. He had driven the money-changers out of the Temple because they represented the destructive and exploitative aspects of what Temple worship had become. He continued to claim that he spoke with the authority of God himself.

The city was full of pilgrims commemorating the liberation of the people of Israel from slavery in Egypt. The religious leaders, allowed by the occupying Romans to have a measure of self-government, were not in the mood for someone claiming to be king, while Jesus' claims to be divine were completely appalling. The Romans must not be provoked, the importance of the Temple must be protected, the people must be quietened. Of course Jesus must die, but how do we do it? How do we get hold of him at night when he is not among the crowds?

We do not know if the religious leaders approached Judas or he approached them. At some point in the discussions it was decided that thirty pieces of silver should be on the table.

On Thursday night he shows them where Jesus is. A kiss is the sign. Jesus is arrested and held until he could be brought next morning to Pilate, the Roman Governor, who had the power to authorise an execution. Thirty silver coins, well spent.

That night Judas will come to a shattering realisation of the terrible thing he has done. But in the same way that he had not registered Jesus' teaching about money he had not truly heard the words about forgiveness and reconciliation and so he despairs. Unlike the lost son in Jesus' story, he does not turn his face to go back home.

And then, he discovers that his new-found friends are not friends at all; they have no interest in him and no concern for his regret. Their contempt is palpable. He has betrayed his friend for money. Greed has become bigger than love. Did he really think they would think highly of him?

But perhaps they were not feeling too good about themselves, either. They are the religious guardians of the chosen people of God. They have offered money for someone to betray a friend. They have handed Jesus, a fellow Jew, to the pagan Romans. They have lied and manipulated. They have been very clever, but they could not have felt proud of themselves.

Perhaps.

—36—

John 13:4
(John 13:1-8 for the context)

"And wrapped a towel round his waist"

It is Thursday evening and Jesus wants to wash his friends' feet. It is a job that needs to be done after a long day in Jerusalem, with streets full of tourists, noise and dust. It is the task of a servant. The group has gathered for a meal but it seems that no-one has arranged for the courtesies of welcome to be carried out. This is not a problem, they know each other well and there are other things on their minds. The Passover Feast is nearing its climax. Tension across the city has been growing and has been focused on Jesus. Would he get through the final days of the week without being attacked or arrested? Or was he about to do something powerful and spectacular that would end Roman rule?

Jesus takes off his outer garment, shedding status and dignity as he does so. The outer garment is unnecessary for the task and would be in the way. He wraps a towel round his waist, for decency and practicality. Towels may not look impressive, but they serve the purpose.

And washes the disciples' feet. One by one he goes around the circle.

Their embarrassment is palpable, Peter finds the idea of receiving this washing particularly awkward. Jesus keeps going and makes the wider point that to be part of his community a person needs to be spiritually washed.

Jesus washes Judas' feet. He knows what Judas is about to do, but still he washes his feet,

He then speaks plainly to them all. "Now that I, your Lord and Teacher, have washed your feet, you also should wash one another's feet. I have set you an example that you should do as I have done for you."

It is all too easy to cast our leader in our own image, so that when we say we are following her or him we are in truth simply gratifying our own desires. The disciples were learning that if they are serious about following Jesus then they need to be serious about who he is and what he does.

Perhaps for many years, whenever they saw a servant reach for a towel, those present in the upper room that evening thought of Jesus.

If ever there was someone they were hesitant to serve, perhaps they remembered that Jesus washed the feet of Judas.

If ever there were moments when they

were too proud or embarrassed to receive the serving love of God through other people, they remembered Peter, and if he was in the room, perhaps he shrugged with a smile.

And perhaps they considered the relative different value and importance of outer garments compared with towels.

—37—

"Jesus took bread, gave thanks and broke it"

The feet had been washed, they settled to eat.

Jesus took bread, gave thanks and broke it

He gives thanks for the bread, which will be broken and will thus remind generations that his body was battered and torn the next day on the cross.

He then gives thanks for the cup of wine, the colour and life of which will remind generations that his blood was shed the next day.

This is my body, this is my blood.

It is moving, mysterious and poignant. Expressions and symbols of suffering and sacrifice beyond human understanding. Not only reminders, but somehow expressing… and Jesus *gave thanks*.

Some present at that meal (perhaps the most famous meal in history?) would have been present on the hillside when a boy brought forward his lunch to help feed thousands of hungry adults. It was only five small barley loaves and two small fish. Not much to be thankful for, some might think. Jesus gives thanks for the bread and then gives thanks for the fish. The crowd was hungry, perhaps they would have chosen to wait for something a little more obviously substantial before giving thanks?

Whatever the child had brought, Jesus was going to be thankful for it. And when Jesus is thankful for it, when Jesus breaks it and shares it, there is enough for everyone.

Paul later emphasised thanksgiving as taking a central part in the Christian life. If this is the example that Jesus set, then his followers should take note. And if Jesus is thankful for child's loaves and fish, then he may even be thankful for our gifts, too, however hesitantly offered.

Perhaps in the upper room on that Thursday night, with its electric atmosphere of anticipation and unease (the Passover themes of liberation, Jesus' public provoking of the religious authorities, the quietly dramatic washing of feet, Judas perhaps not quite himself…) people remembered that hillside, and remembered that when Jesus gives thanks, things happen. The thankfulness always leads to sharing. The five thousand were fed on the hillside, the bread of communion is shared daily around the world, and has been for nearly two thousand years.

Jesus was still being thankful, even when faced with the bread that was to be broken, even when he was about to be betrayed, humiliated, tortured and then judicially murdered. He still found time to be thankful for the bread. And the wine.

And perhaps there is something particular in this meal and all it expresses and represents, that Jesus is thankful for.

–38–

John 18:33
(John 18:20-40 for the context)

"Are you the king?"

Asks Pontius Pilate on that fateful Friday in Jerusalem. Jesus was betrayed and arrested the previous night. If he is to be executed, that means a Roman, not a religious trial. And so Pilate, the Roman governor, is asked to sit in judgement on the Friday morning.

We cannot be sure of the tone of voice. Is he wanting to chuckle with Jesus about those (in Pilate's eyes) intense and absurd religious leaders who had dragged him out of bed for this strange 'trial'? Or is the voice harsh, trying to press Jesus into a confession of kingship which will show an assertive spirit against the might of Rome? Or is Pilate simply interested in what Jesus will say about himself?

Jesus perhaps gives an internal wry smile. This has been the question everyone has been asking since the day he was born. Of David's line, in David's town. Visitors from near and far all wondering if this was the long-awaited king, the true king. Herod, disturbed and angry in Jerusalem. In the Christmas narratives, indeed in all the narratives of the life of Jesus, the watermark question on every page is "Is this the king?"

Jesus lacked the profile of a king. He was born to a poor family, became a refugee, did not talk about gaining palaces or war or wealth. Instead he talked about love and lifestyle, about relationships and money, about lust and compassion. He spent a lot of time with those on the fringes. He seriously annoyed the religious establishment, particularly if they were getting in the way of people's response to the love of God. He set high moral standards for his followers while constantly emphasising mercy.

Are you the king of the Jews?

Jesus's reply is blunt: "Is that your own idea or did others talk to you about me?" It all has got very personal: Pilate, do you have the searching heart that you really want to know, or are you just playing games? What do you really think? Not your neighbour or the crowd, what do you think?

They continue talking and Pilate feels instinctively that Jesus is no criminal. Yet he is under pressure from the local leaders, if he does not execute Jesus they will report him to the emperor in Rome for allowing a rabble-rousing, crown-claiming, blasphemer to go free. We know from other historical sources that

Pilate was a bully. Like many bullies he does not withstand pressure well. He gives in, allows the crowd to decide. The crowd is almost certainly hand-picked by Jesus' enemies; this is not the same crowd who cheered Jesus when he entered Jerusalem the Sunday before, riding on a donkey.

And later that afternoon Jesus is crucified. Pilate insists that above his head is nailed the sign "Jesus of Nazareth, the king of the Jews'. The religious leaders are furious; we do not know if Pilate does it to spite them or whether, somewhere deep inside him, he wonders if this may be the truth; or, very differently, his purpose could be to broadcast a warning to the people: no king but Caesar.

That Friday evening it looked as if the question was no longer relevant. All was over.

And then something happens two days later. And then the question begins to be asked in a new and deeper way, with an even greater weight and urgency than ever before. That was Friday, but Sunday's here.

Are you the king?

That's the question.

—39—

*John 21:15 (John 18:15-18,25-27;
21:15-20 for the context)*

"When they had finished eating, Jesus said to Simon Peter..."

Peter probably guessed that some sort of conversation was going to have to happen. On the Thursday evening of Passover week, he had promised loudly that he would never let Jesus down. After Jesus was arrested Peter then lost his nerve and denied three times that he had ever met Jesus.

It is an awful feeling to have let down a friend.

The cataclysmic events of the Friday and then the extraordinary events of the Sunday had caused even Peter's denial to fade into the background.

But there was still unfinished business.

They are back in home territory, back north by the sea of Galilee. Peter is fishing, the profession he knows best. But the night has been unsuccessful and nothing has been caught. As night fades a figure calls out from the shore to try their nets the other side (this may have been quite annoying. "Why not try it *this way?*" is never much fun to hear, especially when one is tired – but there is an echo here of words of Jesus at the very start of his ministry); and they obey. They lower the nets, and many, many fish are caught. Dawn is breaking, the sun is rising, and Peter and John recognise that the man on the shore is Jesus.

Bread and fish are shared and then Jesus turns to Peter. It is time for the conversation that Peter must have guessed was coming.

When they had finished eating, Jesus said to Simon Peter…

Jesus does not explicitly mention the denial but instead asks a question (Jesus always asks questions), "Do you love me?" He asks it three times, perhaps reflecting Peter's three-fold denial; a positive answer to this question is perhaps the greatest protection against falling again to temptation. When we know we love someone we want to do what is right for them. Perhaps also Jesus is making it clear to Peter that a fall does not mean you have to stop the journey and walk away. Hurting a friend does not mean you stop loving. It can be put right and you carry on.

And he gives Peter a task. "Feed my lambs" – look after the flock of which I am the great shepherd. Nourish them, teach them, protect them.

Jesus knew his friend, he knew Peter would be willing to have the conversation. Jesus wants to forgive, restore and empower. He did it with Zacchaeus and he does it with Peter. The consequences of this quiet conversation after breakfast on the beach still reverberate round the world. Peter took the task entrusted to him very seriously and what he was able to do was extraordinary from any historical viewpoint.

And perhaps he was helped by remembering that this conversation happened after Jesus had guided the experienced fishermen to try something new and to do it his way. The disciples were so excited by the successful catch that they counted – 153 fish were caught. And John solemnly includes the number in his account.

From Peter's point of view, it had been rather a good morning.

–40–

Matthew 28:17
(Matthew 28:16-20)

"Some doubted"

We are not told why they doubted. At this majestic climax of Matthew's account of the life of Jesus, when the risen Christ is inspiring and empowering his followers to take his message of love and reconciliation to the whole world, when he is worshipped by those around him, a new and more complete Moses figure looking out from the mountain over the promised land of spiritual life and freedom, Matthew, with typical honesty, notes that "some doubted."

If Jesus were a certain type of modern politician conducting his final rally it is difficult to imagine his spokesperson publicly recording that "some doubted." But Jesus is not a such a person. And the gospel writers are not those sort of spokespeople.

The understanding that people doubt, and that the questions are often thoughtful and valid, is marbled through the different Biblical writings. Those who wrote the Psalms were full of uncertainties; in the New Testament John the Baptist doubts his own earlier belief about Jesus, and Jesus responds graciously and positively. He likewise replies kindly to the plaintive "I do believe, help me overcome my unbelief!" of the desperate father looking for help for his child. He does not dismiss or ignore the doubts of Thomas.

Faith is affirmed and encouraged, but there is plenty of room for doubt and questions among Jesus' followers. Honest doubt is not a problem to a growing faith, pretence is. The pretending to be what they were not was why Jesus reserved some of his strongest words for hypocritical religious leaders.

This insistence in treating people as they are was central to Jesus' relationships. Even Nicodemus, the nervous Pharisee, member of the ruling council, was welcomed, not chided, for coming hesitantly to see Jesus at night. Prior to that Nathaniel had contemptuously said "Nazareth! Can anything good come from there?", but when invited to come and see Jesus for himself, rather than relying on received prejudice, he received a warm welcome, not a scolding.

Jesus treats people as they are, doubts and all. It is both reassuring and challenging. Reassuring because it means people are always welcome if they want to draw near. Challenging because we should be equally as gentle with others, and their doubts, as Jesus is with us.

There is perhaps also a challenge in whether we can rise to the honesty of Matthew and the other writers. They wanted to tell the story, understandably with their different emphases and interests to the fore, but they wanted to be honest, to tell is as they saw it or heard it. They included the difficulties as well as the joys, the unresolved as well as the crystal clear. Here was truth, and there was no need fearfully to gloss over the awkward or uncomfortable. The truth, said Jesus, shall set you free.

So, Matthew might say, let's just write it as it was. No need to gloss over it, no need to hide from it.

–41–

"Silver and gold I do not have"

Said Peter, but he gave the crippled man at the temple gate called 'Beautiful' all the love and power that he felt he had received from Christ, and the man was healed. The ancient Jewish feast of Pentecost, roughly fifty days after Passover, had come and gone, but during it the Spirit of God had filled Jesus' followers in a dramatic way. Peter had preached a dynamic sermon, focusing on the historical events of the death and resurrection of Jesus, and suddenly this little group were being joined by hundreds of others. Peter walked the streets of Jerusalem, teaching and healing.

A lame man asks for money, but is healed instead.

The religious authorities bring in Peter and John. Caiaphas, the high priest, had been deeply involved in bringing Jesus to trial. He must have been somewhat frustrated that within a few months he was having to act against the followers of that unsettling northern preacher. Will Jesus Christ never go away?

Peter, who had lacked the nerve to speak to a servant girl a few weeks before, denying Jesus three times, speaks boldly to Caiaphas: "Rulers and elders of the people! If we are being called to account today for an act of kindness shown to a cripple and are asked how he was healed, then know this, you and all the people of Israel: It is by the name of Jesus Christ of Nazareth, whom you crucified but whom God raised from the dead, that this man stands before you healed."

Caiaphas and the others were faced with the healed paralytic standing in front of them, a cheering crowd in the streets and an unexpectedly eloquent and confident fisherman. Pontius Pilate is not in Jerusalem any more, he is back in his favoured palace by the Mediterranean. Caiaphas is gambling that outside the frenetic Passover week, with the governor absent, he can get away with allowing some minor disturbances surrounding this cult. It will fade soon. Despite these absurd rumours of resurrection, the preacher must still be dead. People will forget. He decides to cut his losses and lets Peter and John go with a warning to stay silent. Peter simply says "We cannot help speaking about what we have seen and heard." Caiaphas senses his power slipping away and releases them anyway. For the time being.

Silver and gold I do not have

The serious spiritual revivals in Christian history at some point involved people making, informally or formally, a vow to renounce something of the material and emotional riches of this world. These people were often supported by those who had not made the same vow, who stayed relatively wealthy but who had committed to use their money for good. But at the heart were people who felt called to be able to say "Silver and gold I do not have".

And in that calling is sacrifice. Whether you are Francis of Assisi, John Wesley or Peter, you are turning your back on a lifestyle that others think you 'deserved', turning your back on a status in a way that meant that others said you were letting people down. You have been lured away. You do not want to get your hands dirty. Who do you think you are that you don't play the game our way?

Silver and gold, titles and honoured seats and places in the procession, have I none. But in the name of Jesus Christ, this is what I can do… Get up and walk. And the man did.

—42—

"(They) laid their clothes at the feet of a young man named Saul"

'They' are the witnesses to the stoning of Stephen and they laid their clothes at Saul's feet. Saul symbolically (and perhaps actually) held the coats for those who authorised and validated the killing of Stephen. Stephen was a leader in the early church, with particular responsibility for those who were in need of food or shelter.

The holding the coats of course does not mean that Saul was directly responsible...

Or does it?

Despite his youth there must have been something commanding and influential about Saul's presence. Why do they choose him to look after their coats? In affirming the action, whether implicitly or explicitly, Saul condones the killing. Perhaps he would have been able to stop the stoning by force of his intellectual weight and his personality. He could have used his presence for graciousness, not hate. He decides not to do so and Stephen dies. Stephen is of no threat to the stability of Jerusalem but his ideas do not fit within the parameters that his accusers have chosen to have.

Stephen was the first Christian to die for his faith. It is a tragic and poignant moment. Hence he is remembered in many churches the day after Christmas day itself.

And Saul bears a significant level of responsibility. It says much about his later friend Luke's integrity that this episode is included in his writings. By the time the account now known as 'Acts' was published, Saul, now known as Paul, was seen as one of the two big players in the early church. This episode was still included in the records, as equally were the failings of Peter.

The death of Stephen, after a show trial by a group of people who had no genuine interest in what he believed or said, is a typical example of injustice and persecution. It seems to have triggered a higher level of hatred in Saul. The narrative continues: "Godly men buried Stephen and mourned deeply for him. But Saul began to destroy the church. Going from house to house, he dragged off both men and women and put them in prison."

Affirming and encouraging destruction and

violence, Saul's hate is spiralling unchecked. It is as if he is is so terrified by this imagined threat that he is losing his reason. We next hear about him travelling north to Damascus, to carry out his persecution there (it is interesting that the new faith had spread this far, this quickly). He seems blinded and obsessed by hate, and the point will shortly dramatically be made to him that he is indeed blind, and he needs to see truth for what it is.

In holding the coats of hate-filled men, Saul was condoning the hate and allowing it to touch his own heart. It is always good to consider our choice of whose coats we hold.

—43—

Acts 8:26
(Acts 8 for the context)

"Go south to the road
– the desert road"

This makes no sense.

Philip had been a central figure in the early church in Jerusalem, one of the seven deacons. After the killing of Stephen, a fellow deacon, the small group of early Christians scattered, Philip ended up in Samaria and "there was great joy in that city" because of his ministry there. And now he apparently hears an angel telling him to go to the desert road.

It makes no sense. You are not going to meet many people on the desert road, the clue is in the name. Philip, you are clearly not playing to your gifts. You are letting people down. Have you gone mad?

Go south to the road – the desert road

And Philip goes.

Perhaps as he goes he wonders if he has misheard or misunderstood or was it just his imagination that he thought he had heard this message? Does he look around, feeling he has wasted all the opportunities and gifts given to him? Perhaps his faith is stronger than that, and he goes willingly and expectantly. We are not told.

And then one person comes along. Just one.

An Ethiopian travelling home from Jerusalem. He is struggling to understand a passage from the Old Testament. Philip is able to help; he chats with the Ethiopian in his chariot for a while. The Ethiopian is interested in, and then drawn to, the message he is hearing. He wants to take another step and so is baptised there and then.

He is influential in the government of Ethiopia. Perhaps he will share his new faith and understanding when he arrives home. But Philip knows none of this when he heads south to the desert road. He feels that this is the route he needs to take and so he will. For him, it is not so much the thought that the ends justify the means, but rather that the means, if handled right, may yet lead to the right ends.

It is a faith moment. All earthly wisdom would have said that it was right to stay in Samaria.

But Philip moved.

And it was important for one person.

Luke writes too soon fully to know why

this one conversation with one person is so significant. He would not have foreseen how the Christian church in Ethiopia survives to this day, and is thus one of the oldest in the world.

—44—

Acts 9:17
(Acts 9:1-19 for the context)

"Brother Saul"

Saul, powerful, persecutor, the enemy. Now sitting in a house in Damascus, blinded, confused and shocked by a dramatic vision.

Ananias, one of those appalling Christians that Saul had come to ruin, has been told by God to visit him. Ananias understandably wrestles with this. This does not feel to be a good or safe idea, but then obediently he goes. He knocks on the door and is shown to where Saul is sitting.

"Brother Saul," begins Ananias.

Had anyone dared called Saul 'brother' in recent times? Even his friends must have been slightly disturbed by his passionate hatred for this bizarre but harmless sect. The man who had calmly looked after the coats of those who had stoned Stephen must have had, to say the least, a certain icy reputation. His words in his letters after his conversion to Christianity still have moments of real ferocity. What he must have been like before his conversion and introduction to the love and forgiveness of Christ we can only guess.

And here was one of the persecuted, calling him 'brother'.

Brother Saul

'Brother' and 'Sister' are deep words, speaking of respect, equality, heritage, affection, unity and loyalty. In the troubled places of the world, genuine commitment to these words would do much to bring peace. In the troubled places of our own lives genuine commitment to these words would transform so many of our homes, schools and workplaces.

Saul hears the greeting and receives it, and the welcome behind it. He does not leap up and demand to be treated with the respect due to his status and authority. He is not only blind, he is broken. He receives the greeting, the prayer and the healing. His vision is restored. Physically and spiritually he is learning to see again.

We hear no more of Ananias. But we know that Paul never forgot him, otherwise Luke would not have known about, and then written about, this meeting. "Brother Saul" was a greeting of courage, love and respect. Perhaps it was part of Paul's healing and restoring journey.

Whatever one's faith position, it can easily be argued that Paul is one of the most influential people in history. Ananias, the first Christian he truly engaged with, opened the conversation by calling him 'brother'.

That may truly have been rather significant.

Chapter —44

—45—

Acts 11:22
(Acts 11:19-30 for the context)

"They sent Barnabas
to Antioch"

And it was a good choice.

When Barnabas is first mentioned in 'Acts', his generosity to the early church is noted. We then hear that he was the one to introduce the converted Saul to the understandably wary apostles and to convince them that the conversion was genuine.

As we have seen with Philip, the ongoing persecution after Stephen's death had caused a scattering of the early church. Where people went they spread the news about Jesus, and a new group sprang up in Antioch, and grew rapidly. Peter and the others still in Jerusalem wondered if they should be delighted or concerned, from a distance it was difficult to know what was going on.

They sent Barnabas to Antioch.

What did Barnabas have that was so useful to

the early church? Whenever there was uncertainty about what was happening, when a steady voice or clear eyes were needed, Barnabas was asked to be involved. He is the person whose counsel you will seek; he is the one whose judgement you will trust.

Luke continues the narrative: "When he arrived and saw the evidence of the grace of God, he was glad and encouraged them to remain true to the Lord with all their hearts." He then goes to Tarsus and brings Saul back to help him in Antioch and they stay for a year. (We learn that it is here in Antioch that the word 'Christian' is first used.) Barnabas is not possessive or precious about things being done in exactly the same way in every context, he recognises that what is in the heart is what counts. Antioch is different to Jerusalem, but he likes what he sees.

The name 'Barnabas' means 'son of encouragement'. Here was someone who had the personal integrity and strength of character to be able to bring genuine encouragement. The motto of the early church leaders (including such giant figures as Peter, James and John, who had been more closely involved with Jesus than anyone else) seems to have been that if Barnabas thinks it is okay, then that is enough for us. This must have meant that Barnabas' encouragement was not of the careless or unthinking kind. He wanted to believe the best in people but he was not naïve;

if he had been so, his judgement would not have been so trusted.

And it seems he was also a person of some stature and presence – it was even wondered at Lystra if he were the Greek God Zeus, while Paul the great communicator (and, some traditions have it, much shorter) was seen as Mercury. This was unsettling at the time but probably raised some wry smiles back in Jerusalem when the story was recounted.

We know Barnabas is robust. The friendships in the early church were marked by occasional disagreements as well as deep loyalty. Barnabas' particular argument with Paul was serious. Paul felt that John Mark had let him down and that it was too much of a risk to take him again on another missionary journey. Barnabas was not so sure and wanted to give the young man a second chance. He does not give way.

They sent Barnabas to Antioch

Many times his friends must have been thankful that Barnabas was part of the team, perhaps they also wondered what it is that makes a person this trustworthy.

—46—

Acts 20:28
(Acts 20:13-38 for the context)

"Keep watch over

yourselves"

It was a journey of about fifty miles from Ephesus to Miletus. Paul had a rushed timetable as he prepared to go to Rome. After several years of travelling round Mediterranean, focussing on what would now be called Turkey and Greece, he, as a Roman citizen, had exercised his right to defend himself against his accusers in Rome. But he felt there was enough time to arrange a farewell meeting with the leaders of the church of Ephesus.

They travel south to Miletus and meet their mentor and friend. Paul speaks about the need for the leaders to keep watch over their congregations, to remember the value of each person in their church, how much Christ loves each one ('bought with his own blood') and to guard against false teaching, which, wolf-like, can tear apart a fellowship.

But his first command is to "keep watch over themselves." He is reminding them that their own spiritual, emotional, moral and physical welfare is foundational to their ministry to others. They are to watch over themselves as they are to watch over the needs of others.

At the end of the meeting "they all wept as they embraced him and kissed him." There was clearly genuine affection towards this awkward, loving, acerbic, complicated figure. Paul was, to say the least, never a man to seek to win friends by excessive niceness, but his intellectual brilliance, enthusiasm and whole-hearted commitment to people and their spiritual welfare seems to have been inspirational.

As the leaders returned home perhaps they shared memories of Paul's time in Ephesus, of the trouble he had got into when the local souvenir makers had seen a sudden reduction in sales of their little statues of the goddess Diana.

Perhaps they pondered together on what it might mean to "keep watch over themselves", perhaps discussing their own spiritual and emotional needs and suggesting some form of mutual accountability.

It is easy for leaders to become too proud to think they need to think about their own spiritual health. It is easy consciously or unconsciously to leave the searching personal questions for another day, or to think that the usual rules do not apply.

When Paul reaches Rome he is imprisoned and from there he writes a letter to the church in Ephesus. It is full of encouragement and challenge. He talks about the overwhelming love of God 'rich in mercy.' He writes about 'the incomparable riches of his grace,' makes a plea for unity and asks them to stand firm, dressed in the right attitudes and faith; perhaps he is looking at a nearby Roman guard as he describes wearing suitable 'armour of God.'

The leaders of the church in Ephesus would not have travelled to Miletus if they had not liked Paul. They would then have been glad to receive the letter from Rome. The importance of relationship, of affection and friendship, in this community is very evident.

As was the importance of the challenge to leaders to keep watch over themselves.

And Paul wanted to spell it out in his final meeting with them. Proper care for themselves is to be a priority.

—47—

Revelation 1:9
(Revelation 1:1-9 for the context)

"On the island of Patmos"

Did anyone think it would come to this? The young man who had been so close to Jesus, who had sat at Jesus' side at the Last Supper, who had been entrusted from the cross itself with looking after Mary, who had outrun Peter to the empty tomb, who had been a key figure in the early church, is now an old man in exile on Patmos, a small and lonely island between Greece and Turkey. Some historians think it was used by the Romans as a penal settlement. He is there "because of the word of God", implying that his faithfulness to the teachings of Jesus had led him to this punishment. It is all over.

But John is continuing to say his prayers - "he is in the Spirit on the Lord's day" – and receives a serious of visions which includes specific instructions to seven Christian communities, a dramatic interpretation of the age-old struggle between good and evil, and concludes with strong messages of comfort and hope that, when

Christ's return is complete, death and mourning will be no more and there will be a new heaven and earth.

His letter would go out to beleaguered Christians, scattered and persecuted by the Romans. Paul and Peter are dead by now; it is likely that John is the last one living of those close contemporaries of Jesus. It all looks as if the story might be ending.

Except that it is not.

John brings a message of challenge and encouragement and a firm assurance that right will triumph.

On the island of Patmos

Being in exile did not mean for John staring down at the dust and the sand of the island, but rather looking up at the spiritual reality that to his eyes was far more strong and deep than the pressures of this temporal Roman empire. And in so doing he had a vision which included words of the risen Christ which brought comfort to him, no doubt to others at the time when his account was distributed and to countless millions since. Among them this promise, specifically to the church in Laodicea but offered to be shared more widely: "Here I am, I stand at the door and knock, if anyone hears my voice and opens the door, I will come in and eat with them and they with me." Did John think back to Zacchaeus in Jericho when he heard those words?

"It is done. I am the Alpha and the Omega, the Beginning and the End." Did John think back to that stunning exchange Jesus had with the Pharisees when he said "Before Abraham was, I am."?

"To those who are thirsty I will give to drink without cost from the spring of the water of life." Did John think back to an encounter Jesus had with a woman from Samaria where the conversation turned to living water? Did he think back to his history and Acsah getting down from her donkey and asking her father Caleb for springs of water?

Renewed words echoing old memories. An old man pondering and praying. Seeing himself as being still part of it all, and knowing more than most that the calling is not always easy: "I, John, your brother and companion in the suffering and kingdom and patient endurance that are ours in Jesus, was on the island of Patmos…"

Even on Patmos you can dream dreams that change the world.

—48—

Afterword: From
Eden to Patmos

An unspoken challenge in the above list of phrases is that, for most people who came across them, they would have been heard and remembered, not read. In parts of our world the skill of memorising has faded, the words are always available on the page or the screen. For much of history the words would have been learnt, and that makes them much easier to call to mind: they are being called direct from the memory to the present, the route is quicker; there is no need to switch on or to scan the shelves. If we are to follow in the footsteps of the writers referenced in this book we would do well to consider how well we can learn and remember Bible verses.

Alongside this was their ability to be alert to possibilities. It is intriguing how quotations from the early scriptures are used by the later writers of scriptural texts. There is an exuberance and freedom in their approach as they seize upon an aspect of an old saying and appropriate it to their context. Their desire to play around with ideas, to follow the thought home, to see 'what we can make of this', is as inspirational as their ability to memorise.

But perhaps the biggest challenge is their understanding that these words could be relevant. These were not phrases simply to be pondered, learnt, explored and debated. These were words to affect how we would talk to the market-stall holder, stay standing firm when the clouds are gathering, be thoughtful as we pray, love, play, read and forgive, or when we open our purse. These words mattered. Saturday morning in the synagogue, Sunday morning in the churches, were important, but the next afternoon or day in the workplace or the home was what really counted.

Aged John knew Lamentations by heart, and would have been aware of the power and relevance of the words as he sat on Patmos. As he sketched his memories of his extraordinary vision of Christ triumphant and of his belief that all, finally, will be well, perhaps occasionally these words flitted through his mind:

Yet this I call to mind, and therefore I have hope.

Index of Old Testament Passages

Index of New Testament passages

Luke 17:15	"One of them, when he saw he was healed, came back"	101
Luke 19:5	"Zacchaeus"	107
Matthew 1:19	"(He) did not want to expose her to public disgrace"	76
Matthew 2:8	"So that I too may go and worship him"	79
Matthew 14:8	"Give me the head of John the Baptist"	86
Matthew 25:8	"Our lamps are going out"	113
Matthew 26:15	"So they counted out for him thirty silver coins"	116
Matthew 26:26	"Jesus took bread, gave thanks and broke it"	122
Matthew 28:17	"Some doubted"	131
Revelation 1:9	"On the island of Patmos"	152